Flute

FMX 28/4/10
FOZ 20/7/10
LMX 29/12/10

YEHUDI MENUHIN MUSIC GUIDES

Bassoon by William Waterhouse
Cello by William Pleeth
Clarinet by Jack Brymer
Early Music by Denis Stevens
Flute by James Galway
Horn by Barry Tuckwell
Oboe by Leon Goossens and Edwin Roxburgh
Organ by Arthur Wills
Percussion by James Holland
Piano by Louis Kentner
Saxophone by Paul Harvey
Trumpet by Crispian Steele-Perkins
Violin and Viola by Yehudi Menuhin and William Primrose
Voice edited by Keith Falkner

Flute

James Galway

KAHN & AVERILL, LONDON

This edition first published in 1990 by
Kahn & Averill
9 Harrington Road, London SW7 3ES

First published in Great Britain in 1982 by
Macdonald & Co Ltd

Reprinted 1992, 1994, 1996, 1999

British Library Cataloguing in Publication Data

Galway, James, *1939-*
    Flute. - (Yehudi Menuhin music guides; no. 2)
    1. Concert flutes. Concert flute music. Concert flutes &
    concert flute music to 1980
    I. Title II. Series
    788.3193

    ISBN 1-871082-13-7

Printed in Great Britain by
Halstan & Co Ltd., Amersham, Bucks

Contents

Part Two
PLAYING, PRACTISING AND DEVELOPING TECHNIQUE

Illustrations

Acknowledgements

I would not have been able to consider writing a book such as this had I not been fortunate enough to have a succession of excellent teachers, to all of whom I give my grateful thanks. Those who had the most profound influence on me were Muriel Dawn and Billy Dunwoody in Belfast, and in London, John Francis at the Royal College and Geoffrey Gilbert at the Guildhall School. In Paris, Jean-Pierre Rampal provided great inspiration and occasional lessons and in later life periodic visits to the legendary Marcel Moyse have helped me to crystallize my personal philosophy of flute playing.

When you spend as much time on the road as I do, help from assistants, publishers and others is indispensable. I could not have begun to write this book without the invaluable help of Elena Duran who was my assistant at the time. Penny Hoare has proved to be the most patient of midwives, whilst Yehudi Menuhin and Patrick Jenkins provided constant encouragement. Eric Fenby, who discovered my desire to venture into print, has consistently offered both good advice and practical help.

Maureen McConville, Hugh Young, Henry Raynor, Jacob Mayne, Kathy Nicholson and Alex Weekes have all assisted in putting order into the text whilst my friend and manager, Michael Emmerson, who claims never to have put a flute to his lips, has lived through it all.

Preface
by Yehudi Menuhin

Of all the sounds created by the human being, the sound of the flute is the purest. The clarity of the notes it produces is for me an ideal voicing of the natural simplicity all music is forever striving to achieve. The flute has the extraordinary capacity to transport us into realms unsullied by strife or anger – the mood the flute evokes for me is one of yearning, of philosophical regret, but it is a regret purified of bitterness. No wonder Hippocrates counselled the sounds of a shepherd's flute in convalescence to heal body and mind.

James Galway is a most fitting guide to the intricacies and delights of this most ancient of instruments with its aerial flights and figures and its note of inner serenity and compassion. Certainly he writes out of a remarkable richness of experience as well as a clear desire to communicate with those who come to study his chosen instrument. 'Music', James Galway writes, 'is a language'. And although he is disarmingly modest about his ability to communicate in words I have no doubt that the reader will find in his very full and detailed text the same warmth and enthusiasm those fortunate enough to have heard him play will know that he brings to his performances. Certainly he has revolutionized the whole concept of the flute and its music and his dedication to, and delight in, the instrument will communicate itself immediately to all who read his book.

Part One

The Flute

No one knows how, when or where the flute was invented. Certainly it was developed many centuries, probably many millennia, before writing music was thought of, so that when this or that culture took to keeping records and recording history, nobody was in a position to remember how the flute was first thought up. There it was, part of the essential furniture of life.

What can be said without fear of error is that every culture, every country, every part of the world has produced flutes of one sort or another and usually of several. Dig into the past where you will and there you find someone with a flute. There has never been a people anywhere, at any stage of the history of mankind, for whom flutes were not important.

They were the first instruments. I say this confidently, in the absence of contrary evidence. True, one perverse opinion holds that possibly some primitive form of drum came first; someone hit something, found it made a noise, and took up hitting things as a profession. If you want to go along with that argument, so be it. Neither of us is likely to find conclusive proof to silence the other. But for my money, the flute comes first.

Not only was it the first instrument, it was, and remains, the most natural. The sound comes from inside the body, in a way not possible with instruments to be hit or scraped. It is an extension of the player's speaking and singing voice. His breath, his muscles, his fingers produce the sound, without intervening technical complications. Nothing separates him from the tone, no mechanism, no reed, no hammer, no bow nor string. Only singers have less paraphernalia between them and their listeners. You just put your lips to the flute and blow. Hopefully the result is music.

But what *is* music? Basically music is sound, but there are other parts to the answer. The sound has to be beautiful. Not only does it have to be beautiful, it has to say something. Music is communication, it is a language. If I am more eloquent in that language than in printed English, I hope you will excuse me. A large part of my life has been spent in learning how to communicate in the language of music. The language of speech has had to shift for itself, which, I suggest, is pretty much the experience of most of us. What command of words I have is now at the service of music, the flute and the learner. I hope my words will lead the reader back to the language of music.

Let's begin by considering how the first and most natural of instruments learned to speak to the human race.

One
The Beginnings

Given the all-pervasiveness of flutes in ancient history, I think we can only conclude that they were invented many times over by a great number of separate and inspired people. Perhaps discovered is a better word than invented. At its most basic, the flute is practically an accident – any old hollow stick, reed or length of cane that happens to be lying around. The creative human part of the operation is what turns this disregarded piece of kindling into a vehicle for musical communication, of course. That is where the discovery or the invention comes in.

What a flute is

Essentially, the flute is a hollow tube blown, without reed, in such a way that the air enclosed inside it vibrates. Everything to be said in the following pages, all the refinements that have gone into the modern instrument, do not alter this fundamental truth. A hollow tube in which the air vibrates is what you and I play today.

But across the centuries and the continents the flute has cropped up in some pretty diverse forms. Behind this variety lies the fact that there is more than one way of blowing the flute in order to produce vibrations. What all ways have in common is that the air stream is broken on a sharp edge. Some flutes are held vertically and produce a note when the air is blown across the open top so that it hits the further side of the rim. These 'end-blown' flutes sometimes have a notch cut in the rim to assist the sound. Flageolets, or fipple flutes, of which the recorder is an

The Flute

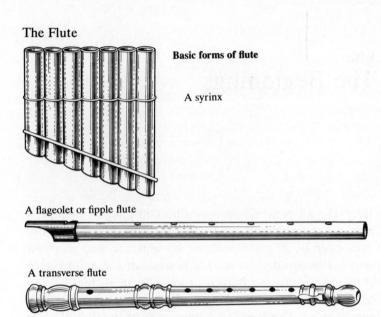

Basic forms of flute

A syrinx

A flageolet or fipple flute

A transverse flute

example, are blown through a mouthpiece with a duct, the 'fipple', inside the tube to direct the air against a hole cut in the side of the tube. On transverse flutes, the sort of flutes I shall chiefly be writing about, the essential feature is a hole cut in the side of the tube close to one end. The player directs the air stream across the hole in order to bounce it off the sharp edge on the far side and make it vibrate. Some flutes in the Pacific Islands are blown by air from the nose, but we won't trouble to explore that particular bypath.

So far we have a hollow tube capable of producing a single note. Hot on the heels of this achievement comes another discovery: the shorter the pipe, the higher the note. Bind a few pipes together in graded lengths and you have the panpipes or syrinx and are in the music-making business – effective but cumbersome. The essential breakthrough was to have one pipe produce several notes by cutting finger holes in it which could be stopped when not needed. Wagner attributed this discovery to Siegfried, the dragon-killer. The truth is that the ability to draw acoustical conclusions from the evidence to hand was pretty widely spread around the human race.

Flutes in the ancient world

The Old Testament tells us that Jubal was the father of all who play upon the harp and pipe. A little more detail about the harps and pipes would have been welcome, but Scripture remains terse on the subject and Biblical scholars today hesitate to say just what these instruments were like. Somewhat more enlightenment comes from other parts of the ancient Near East, from Sumeria and Egypt, but most of the information is pictorial and so not as exact as we could wish. These civilizations had a cane pipe, rim-blown, about a yard long, without holes at first but later with as many as three or four holes; flutes buried in Egyptian tombs demonstrate a three-holed variety. The instrument seems to have begun as a shepherd's pipe and to have been co-opted later for religious ceremonial.

The Greeks seem to have been the first to use six finger holes, so that their instruments could play every note of the mode or scale in which they were tuned. Actually the Greeks favoured reed pipes above reedless ones. The flute was for shepherds, villagers and the uncultivated in general. The *aulos*, forerunner of the oboe, was the one with prestige, and this sorry state of affairs lasted until the Middle Ages, when flutes came into their own in Northern Europe. Meanwhile of course the people played merrily away, not greatly caring whether the flute was highly regarded or not.

Folk flutes

There is hardly a people in the world today, primitive or developed, that doesn't play some sort of flute. End-blown flutes range from six-foot monsters in New Guinea to the 'Bushman's flute' in Africa, made from an ostrich quill. Flageolets are found in one form or another pretty well everywhere. In Java they have one called the *suling* which is played with their famous *gamelan* percussion bands. The North American Indians have the Apache flute; a rather cumbrous instrument nicknamed the 'lover's flute'. We have our own folk flageolet, too. When I played one as a kid it was called a penny whistle, but since then it's been overtaken by inflation.

India and Japan are great flute-playing countries. The Hindus' god Krishna is often represented playing a transverse flute with finger holes, known as a *murli*. The name *bansari* is given to several kinds of flute. Originally it meant one made of bamboo (*banse* means bamboo), a simple instrument with a range of under two octaves, some end-blown but some, like the *murli*, side-blown. Nowadays the *bansari* has gone up in the world, and many are made of metal. You can hear them in Indian classical music and in the film music that is so popular all over India.

Japanese classical music, like so much of Japanese art, is closely bound up with tradition. The court orchestras that play the *gagaku* ('elegant music') for the *bunraku* dances have two kinds of flute, the *hichiriki*, a flageolet with nine holes, and a transverse flute. By tradition the 'left-hand music' has a flute with seven holes and the 'right-hand music' one with six holes. The Japanese also have a beautiful end-blown, slightly notched, flute, the *shakuhachi*. Its four holes give it the pentatonic scale, D F G A C, characteristic of Japanese music, but other notes can be produced by overblowing and cross-fingering. The tone of the *shakuhachi* is absolutely enchanting.

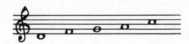

Europe takes over

For the first thousand years of the Christian era, Europe was backward in comparison with Byzantium and the East. Progress, learning, luxury all derived from the Orient. So also did music and musical instruments. The first flute to go West was the simple pipe played with the tabor. It arrived in Europe in the first half of the twelfth century. The pipe, a front-blown flute, had three finger holes – two in front, one at the back for the thumb – and was played with one hand. The other hand beat the rhythm on the tabor. The legs were free for dancing. As you may imagine, this flute had still not travelled far up-market, but its arrival marked the beginning of the flute's acceptance as a respectable instrument worthy of the attention of proper composers. The pipe player achieved a scale by over-blowing to reach the second and third harmonics of the notes stopped: C, D, E and F were second harmonics, G, A, B and C were third harmonics.

At about the same time two other varieties of flute were gaining ground. Eastern Europe exported the transverse flute to Germany, where it was established by the twelfth century; in the fifteenth century, in the form of the fife played along with a drum, it was widely played both for military purposes and for jollification. Meanwhile flageolet-type instruments were moving from south to north. These were fipple flutes, like the recorder, which in the fourteenth century came into general use as an improvement on similar instruments of the past.

The recorder was to have a long innings.

Two
The Recorder

Henry Bolingbroke, later to become Henry IV of England, had his household accounts drawn up for the year 1388 when he still went by the title Earl of Derby. Included in the inventory was i (meaning one) *fistula nomine ricordo*, a pipe called a recorder, seemingly the first use of what became the common name for this instrument.

During the centuries of its popularity, from the fourteenth to the mid-eighteenth, it acquired a few other names: the *flûte á bec*, on the grounds that the mouthpiece resembled a beak, the *flûte douce*, because of the serenity of its tone, the 'English flute', because the English took to it with such enthusiasm. For a time, while its final form was still evolving, it was known as the *flûte á trois trous*, a name which clung to it even after it had gained the six finger holes of the modern instrument. And there were other names which we can afford to ignore.

What is even more confusing than our forefathers' habit of having six names for one instrument is their habit of having one name for six instruments. By the seventeenth century, half the time when they said 'flute' they meant 'recorder', and when they said 'pipe', they could be referring to any high-voiced woodwind instrument that happened to be at hand. Hamlet, in Shakespeare's play, offers a recorder to Guildenstern with the invitation 'Will you play upon this pipe?' Purcell in the seventeenth century called the recorder 'the flute', though in 1668 (when Purcell was nine) Samuel Pepys wrote in his diary that he had bought a recorder. By 1780, the learned historian of music Dr Burney was mystified by the name recorder, although, under the title 'the common flute', he knew the instrument perfectly well. When Handel or Bach wrote 'flute' or 'flauto' they meant treble recorder. If they wanted a transverse flute they said so.

The evolution of the recorder

In 1511, in a book about musical instruments dedicated to the Bishop of Strasbourg, Sebastian Virdung illustrated his entry on the recorder with an engraving which, though rather hit-and-miss, shows the instrument more or less as we know it today. So by the beginning of the sixteenth century the recorder had completed its evolution.

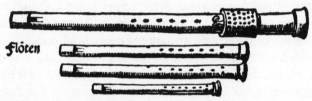

Consort of recorders from Virdung's *Musica Getuscht*, 1511

By that time, too, the recorder had a great public and social pretensions, but it began as a low class instrument of the people, and most of the important stages in its evolution occurred during this plebeian part of its career.

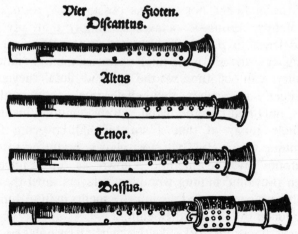

Consort of recorders from Agricola's *Musica Instrumentalis*, 1528

9

Early recorders (like early transverse flutes, for that matter) were cut from single lengths of wood, but it was soon discovered that the central bore of the windway could be made more effective if the instrument came in two pieces, a body and a foot, the foot having a joint which slid into the body.

Even sooner must have occurred the technical advance which makes the recorder what it is: the insertion of the fipple, or blockage, in the mouthpiece, which closes the head, leaving only a narrow windway through which air is directed against the 'lip', the bevelled edge of the air vent.

Finger holes came a little later, although still before the recorder's elevation to high society. When it still belonged to folk music it was given three finger holes and played in the same manner as the taborer's pipe. By the time Henry Bolingbroke listed one among his household goods, it had acquired seven holes, the six regular holes and a thumb hole at the back of the pipe, near its foot, to make it easier for the player to manage the over-blown second octave.

Early fifteenth-century recorder (in the Gemeente museum, The Hague)

With six finger holes it was possible to produce two completely chromatic octaves so simply that any child could learn to do it. Problems remained, however: too strong a breath drove the pitch upwards, too light a one let it collapse into flatness. If the holes were too large, they produced flat notes, if too small sharp ones. Correctly cut holes, only half covered, would give a semitone instead of a whole tone, so that a sort of half-covering finger technique was useful, but most players preferred to make semitones by the method known as 'cross-fingering' which prevailed among woodwind players until the mid-nineteenth century and the improvements in flute-building introduced by Theobald Boehm.

Cross-fingering works like this: with all six holes covered, a pipe plays its lowest note, normally, in the early days, D. Uncover the lowest hole (that is, the one furthest from the mouthpiece) and the sound is raised a tone, to E. Uncover, two finger holes, and the note produced is again a tone higher, F#, though not exactly in tune. If F♮ is required, the lowest hole must be covered and the second hole uncovered. G is played by uncovering the three lowest holes. Now cover the bottom two holes, and G is flattened to F#. The same method is used to produce the upper half of the scale, with the D, E, F and G note-holes covered. A opens the fourth hole and B the fifth, but B♭ can be obtained by opening the fourth and fifth holes, C# by opening the sixth, but C♮ by opening both fifth and sixth. In short, to open two adjacent holes lowers the tone of the upper one by a semitone. As already mentioned, the second octave is produced by over-blowing.

Two features may account for the recorder's long years of glory.

First, in an age of amateur music, it was the ideal instrument. It had no mechanisms to go wrong; the player did not need to learn some special embouchure, he simply put the mouthpiece between his lips and blew.

Secondly, there was appeal in the calm purity of its tone, which did not vary whatever the mood of the music and could not be greatly influenced by anything the player did. The simplicity of the sound, apparently without harmonics or overtones, seemed to owe nothing to knowledge, mechanism, or even the skill of the player. There are grounds for saying that, while the flute is the most natural of instruments, the recorder is the most natural of flutes.

Recorders in consort

Precisely because of the character of the sound, the recorder lacked a little something as a solo instrument, however. This did not trouble our forefathers. Instrumental polyphony was the in thing in the fifteenth century, 'consorts' of instruments (as they were called) were the pop-groups of the day. So the next stage in the recorder's evolution was its appearance in varying sizes, three or four of which could perform together, each with a different voice taking a different part, like singers. The basic instrument was the treble recorder. Higher pitched were the descant (or soprano) and the sopranino or exilent, lower pitched the tenor, the bass, and just occasionally for the heavy stuff, the great bass.

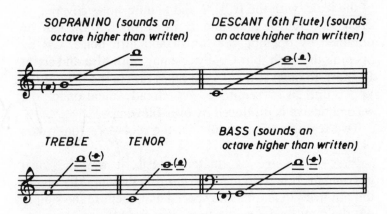

SOPRANINO *(sounds an octave higher than written)* DESCANT *(6th Flute) (sounds an octave higher than written)*

TREBLE TENOR BASS *(sounds an octave higher than written)*

In the later sixteenth century the following were also made:

DESCANT *(3rd Flute) (an octave higher than written)* ALTO ALTO TENOR

With all these voices, the recorder family reproduced virtually the entire range of a human choir, but – and this was the recorder's special contribution to ensemble playing – with a complete homogeneity of tone from lowest to highest tessitura.

from a Thomas Morley *Air*

Philip, Duke of Burgundy from 1419 to 1467, heard a
quartet of *fleute* (i.e. recorder) players in 1437, two of the
instruments probably being trebles, two tenors, for another
generation had to pass before the bass voice and the
register in which it operated were taken seriously. By the
next century, a typical consort would consist of a treble,
two tenors (one acting as alto) and a bass. When Henry
VIII died in 1547, his musical instruments were listed. The
inventory shows that he possessed seventy-two flutes and
seventy-six recorders, grouped in consorts but with the
bass recorders listed separately.

King Henry is almost as well-known for his passion for
music as for his passion for marrying, but he was far from

alone in collecting instruments and giving employment to musicians. All through the Tudor period, the number of woodwind and string players in royal service increased, and the names of a few players have survived. Elizabeth I had a flute player called Guys and a couple of recorder players, Lanier and Paker. In addition she had six shawm players at her disposal, all of whom, like Guys, would be capable of handling a recorder should occasion demand it. Below court level too, music flourished in England. The Kytson family of Kengrave Hall in Suffolk were a musical bunch. In the early seventeenth century they employed the great madrigalist John Wilbye as resident composer for family entertainments, and of course they amassed musical instruments, among them a case of seven recorders, all probably differently pitched, and a couple of 'flewtes' – the real thing, this time. But long years had yet to pass before the flute ousted the recorder.

The seventeenth and eighteenth centuries

What saw the recorder finally off the scene was the development of the classical orchestra in the eighteenth century. For orchestral as opposed to ensemble playing, the recorder was not well equipped, perhaps because its evolution had come to an end. The instrument that Bach knew was in almost every respect the same as the ones which Philip of Burgundy and Henry VIII had heard, and for that matter the same as the instruments played today by countless school children. No steps were taken to enlarge its two-octave range or to increase its limited dynamic power.

But during all this time it remained simple, accessible and popular all over Europe. In England the name recorder fell into disuse; the instrument did not. Samuel Pepys already played the flageolet (the French version of the English descant recorder, with a spherical bulge under its mouthpiece) when, on 27 February 1668, he went to see a play called *The Virgin Martyr*. He didn't think much of the play, but was 'ravished' by its 'wind musique', and promptly bought a recorder for himself and another for his wife. Until late in the seventeenth century, popular songs were sold with a recorder part printed beneath the voice and bass music.

Bach's orchestra, whether in Weimar, Cöthen or Leipzig, clearly disposed of both recorders and flutes, for he always took care to specify which of them he wanted. The direction *flauto* or *flûte-á-bec* in his scores means the treble recorder; the modern flute he referred to as *flauto traverso*, or, in French, *flûte traversière*, more rarely in German as *Traversflöte* or *Querflöte*. Transverse flutes are indicated on his scores only after his visit to Dresden in 1730. The presumption is that, in the opera house there, it was the first time he heard the flute played impressively.

Bach never scored for flute and recorder together, probably because they were played by the same musicians. The players who lamented on recorder for the Gethsemane meditation in the *St. Matthew Passion* were the same people whose *flauti traversi* added sniggering comments to the chorus *Lasst ihn kreuzigen* at the trial of Christ in the same oratorio.

But these versatile fellows were not professionals from the town team of *Stadtpfeifer*, or waits. In 1730 Bach found it necessary to send a memo to the Leipzig town council, his employers, pointing out that he depended on university students or on boys from his own choir school for such instruments as flutes, so essential in modern music.

The Flute

Although Bach mainly used recorders for special effects, he did include them in the orchestration of the Second and Fourth Brandenburg Concertos, written at Cöthen before his appointment to Leipzig. As we shall see, a great deal more important work was entrusted by him to the flute, which he wrote for in the Fifth Brandenburg.

Like Bach, Handel wrote for both types of flute, and like Bach, he specified which he wanted, scoring for 'German' – that is, transverse – flute to distinguish it from the recorder. His Italian cantatas provide some very attractive recorder music, but perhaps his most famous writing for this instrument is the sparkling comic obbligato for the sopranino recorder to Polyphemus's aria 'O ruddier than the cherry' in *Acis and Galatea*. Here the incongruity between the singer's bumbling bass and sopranino's piping is exploited delightfully.

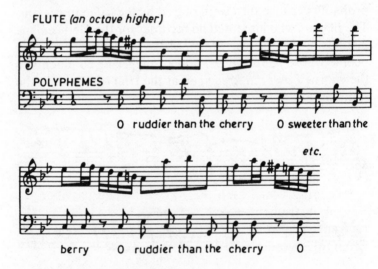

Handel's principal oboe player until 1730, the Belgian Jean-Baptiste Loeillet, was credited in his own day with being the first musician to play the German flute in England. This is certainly not literally true, but Loeillet may well have been the first to play it at public concerts to a paying audience. However that may be, he did a great deal to popularize it, in compositions and in performance. He gave weekly concerts at his home to fashionable audiences, the other players being amateurs of some social standing who, according to Sir John Hawkins's *General History of the Science and Practice of Music*, 'gratified him very handsomely for his assistance in conducting them'. In other words, they paid dearly for the privilege.

Loeillet helped spell the recorder's doom, but he still played it and wrote for it. Among his important compositions are sets of sonatas for recorder and continuo and a number of pieces in which recorders are combined with oboe and strings. When he died his place as the outstanding flute player of the day was taken by another Continental immigrant, Carl Friedrich Weideman, who came to England about 1726 and died in 1782. But where Loeillet was associated with both kinds of flute, Weideman was strictly a transverse flute man, as player and composer.

For the recorder, the writing was definitely on the wall.

The last composer to write extensively for the recorder was Telemann, a lot of whose work was destined for amateur musicians in Hamburg. It ranges from cheerful, friendly, gossipy stuff, as of a man with nothing important to say, to music of compelling power and depth. Telemann died in 1767. Only a few years later the German composer, organist and poet, C. F. D. Schubart, wrote the recorder's epitaph: 'This instrument has now almost fallen out of use because of its quiet tone and limited compass.'

Its eclipse lasted until the twentieth century, when the English instrument maker Arnold Dolmetsch launched a revival. Meanwhile the transverse flute had more than taken the recorder's place.

Three
Development of the Flute

Almost two centuries before Telemann's death, in 1599 to be exact, a prophetic word had been spoken of the flute. In that year Thomas Morley published the first music specifically written for 'broken consorts', that is, groups of different instruments rather than groups of the same instrument in different sizes. The flute, declared this discriminating gentleman, combined better with strings than did the recorder, and he thereupon wrote his six-part *Consort Lessons* for two viols, three lutes of different pitch, and, preferably, a flute. But the recorder's hold was still sufficiently strong for Morley to allow it as an alternative candidate for the sixth part. (Incidentally, Morley used the word 'lesson' in the same spirit as Chopin used the word 'study' – fun to play, fun to hear, but obliging musicians to face up to particular difficulties.)

Flutes were, of course, also played in consort, as we can deduce from Henry VIII's inventory. The normal consort consisted of a treble, a tenor (the instrument nearest our own flute) and a bass. With their heavier tone, and played largely in their lower register, they must have made a splendidly rich sound.

However, the flute was a great deal more difficult to play. The player must do with his lips all those things which a recorder's mouthpiece, fipple and narrow windway do automatically for the recorder player. A recorder player can be a superlative musician, his intonation absolutely spot on, his music phrased with elegance and eloquence, but he cannot add to his instrument's capacity for simple utterance. In contrast the flute has a range of interesting, attractive colours, powerful dynamics, and a compass extending from an ominous hollow sound at the bottom to a fierce cutting edge at the top. Whereas the recorder is monochromatic, the flute is capable of great expressiveness, but – and here comes the crunch – its expressiveness depends entirely on the skill of the player.

With the help of a skilled player or two, the flute's wider resources and greater expressiveness finally won it acceptance as an orchestral and solo instrument.

French innovations

France set the cultural fashions for the rest of Europe in the seventeenth and eighteenth centuries, so the fact that woodwind music in general, and – increasingly – flute music in particular, were appreciated at the French court had important consequences for countries (and musicians) far and wide.

De la Barre and other musicians attr. Tornière, 1710

The Flute

The story can be said to begin in 1678 when Lully wrote the flute into the score of his ballet, *Le Triomphe de l'Amour*, but behind this emergence into the light of public acclaim lay a series of backroom developments. We know what the flute, or at any rate one flute, was like in the early part of that century, because a scholarly cleric, Marin Mersenne, described what he called 'one of the best flutes in the world' in a book, *Harmonie Universelle*, published in 1637. He also included an engraving to illustrate his text, which disconcertingly shows the instrument to be curved. Whether it had got warped in some way, or something was wrong with the engraving, is not explained. Anyway Mersenne provided a few statistics.

Transverse flute from Mersenne's *Harmonie Universelle*, 1637

The instrument was 23.45 inches long. The mouth hole was 3.2 inches from the head of the flute, 0.71 inch from the end of the stopper. The finger holes varied in size from 0.266 to 0.444 inch. Since the flute was tuned in D, notes in other keys were played either by cross-fingering or by covering the holes only partially. To be within reach of every size of hand, the E and A holes had to be cut above their true position, so that, to correct the sound, they were made smaller than the other holes.

On this flute a good player could achieve two and a half octaves of more or less completely chromatic scales, but this range depended on the management of the embouchure. The air stream for the first octave had to be narrowed to half the width for the second, and halved again for the notes above the second. Clearly it was not an instrument to be entrusted to the clumsy, the cack-handed or those whose intonation was less than exact.

Some years later came a further innovation. Theoretically, the boring of new holes must extend the compass of the instrument, but there were good reasons for not multiplying the number of holes unnecessarily. The size of the average hand was one limitation, the desire to maintain the existing pitch another, the unwillingness to have to rethink the entire fingering system a third. These limitations notwithstanding, in about 1660 the flute gained a new hole, bored half way between the lowest finger hole and the open end of the pipe. Its purpose was to play D# (and of course its harmonics), previously obtainable only by cross-fingering, and never really clear or full-voiced. Occasionally in the past keys had been fitted to flutes (recorders as well as flutes proper) to open and close finger holes beyond the player's reach. This was now done. The D# hole was operated by a key manipulated by the little finger of the right hand. It was held open and closed again by a spring when the key was released.

Another French improvement was to bore the flute conically. By this time the instrument was made in three pieces, a head, a body, and a foot which narrowed from about 0.72 inch where it joined the body to about 0.45 inch at the other extremity. Finger holes were smaller than those described by Mersenne.

Section of baroque flute, showing conical bore

But in spite of the backroom boys, the intonation of the flute remained uncertain. One factor was the material from which it was made. At this time the most popular material was boxwood, which both looks handsome and produces a mellow sweet tone. Boxwood, however, absorbs condensation readily, which causes the wood to swell and puts the intonation entirely out of kilter. An alternative material was ivory, but its touch and texture were unpleasant to the player's lips. Metal flutes had advantages accompanied by drawbacks, one of which was their liability to be affected by the temperature of the room.

Intonation then depended (as to some extent it still depends) on two things, besides the material used. One was the exactitude in the making of the finger holes, the other the flute-player's use of them. From both maker and player the utmost precision was required.

Originally note holes were cut, as with recorders, to suit the natural spread and fall of the fingers of the average hand. The use of large holes enabled the player to correct his intonation within quite broad limits, but the quality of sharp or flat notes made by cross-fingering was very doubtful. After the invention of the D# key, flute makers began to reduce the size of the finger holes so that the intonation would be clearer and more precise, but they still had a long way to go to reach their target.

As late as 1776 Sir John Hawkins wrote: 'The German or transverse flute still retains some degree of estimation among gentlemen whose ears are not nice enough to inform them that it is never in tune.' Mozart, about the same time, is reputed to have disliked the flute for the unreliability of its intonation, though the wonderful music he wrote for it suggests that what he really disliked was not the instrument but the unreliability of run-of-the-mill players. Dr Burney, touring Europe to investigate musical history and listening to all the music he could, travelled from place to place lamenting the tendency of woodwinds to go out of tune. By the time these three gentlemen were making their complaints, the flute was a very different animal from the keyless instrument of before 1660.

Back to the seventeenth century. The new flute, with its conical bore and D# key, may well have been the work of the Hotteterre family in Paris, a father, four sons and a grandson. They played woodwind instruments as skilfully as they made them, are credited with the invention of the oboe and generally wrapped up the French woodwind scene, putting the seal on French predominance.

From the point of view of us flute players, the most important Hotteterre was the grandson, Jacques-Martin, nicknamed 'le Romain' because he spent some time in Rome. His flute playing was so outstanding that not only did Louis XIV give him a principal job in the royal orchestra, but throngs of noblemen became his pupils.

Hotteterre published the first text-book of flute playing, and composed a great deal of music for the instrument. More than any other single player Hotteterre-le-Romain was responsible for the popularity of the flute in eighteenth-century France. In his *History*, Sir John Hawkins gives him the credit of leading upper class France to forsake the recorder in favour of the flute, with the result that the recorder dwindled into being an instrument for 'young apprentices of tradesmen'.

Hotteterre's text-book, *Les principes de la flûte traversière* (1707), is illustrated by pictures of two instruments, made in four sections: a short cylindrical mouthpiece and stopper; a long cylindrical neck; a body with six finger holes, narrowing towards the foot which contains only the D# hole and its key. Each joint was of course a weak spot, so was strengthened with an apparently decorative band, often of ivory.

Illustration from Hotteterre's *Principes de la flûte traversière*, 1707

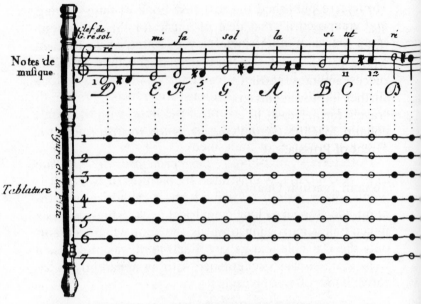

Chart from Hotteterre's *Principes de la flûte traversière*, 1707

Another influential French player was Pierre-Gabriel Buffardin, a native of Marseilles who spread the word and example of French excellence beyond the frontiers. In 1715 he became first flute in the King of Saxony's orchestra in Dresden, and was still in this position when Bach visited the Saxon capital; Bach is thought to have written his A minor Partita for unaccompanied flute for him. For all the evidence suggests that Buffardin's genius rose above the deficiencies of the one-keyed flute. His salary was doubled in 1741, which would seem to be convincing testimony of his market value.

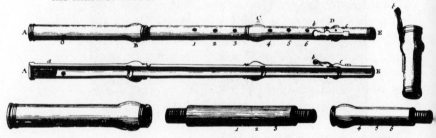

Illustration from Diderot's *Encyclopédie*, with flute divided into four sections

France gave rise not only to technical innovations but also to flute virtuosi and much music for the flute. The three things go together. Better flutes led to better players, whose performance encouraged composers to write more pieces, and more testing pieces. And this in turn prompted further improvements in the instrument. But now the tale travels further east, to a remarkable partnership, that of Johann Joachim Quantz and his employer, Frederick the Great of Prussia.

Johann Joachim Quantz

In this partnership, Quantz was the majority shareholder, at least so far as you and I are concerned. But it was Frederick, no mean musician himself, who made Quantz's contribution possible; and if it hadn't been Frederick, it would likely have been some other monarch, for there was quite a tussle among German princes for the services of this great and innovative flute maker, player and composer.

Musically, Quantz set a standard of accurate intonation which none of his contemporaries lived up to. Structurally, he added another key to the flute, invented a tuning slide to cope with problems of pitch, and brought a new precision to the size of mouth and finger holes. Let us have a look at his widely travelled career.

The son of a blacksmith, Quantz, who was born in 1697 near Göttingen, made an unlikely start for a flute virtuoso: as a child he played the double bass. Musical education in the Germany of his day was acquired by way of apprenticeships to the guilds of town musicians, and as an apprentice Quantz added a few other instruments to his repertory, including the violin and the harpsichord. He had already worked in a couple of cities, Dresden being one, by the time he was twenty, when he went to Vienna to study counterpoint. In 1718 he was appointed oboist in the Polish court chapel, and then or thereabouts he began studying the flute. Naturally he chose to study under the celebrated Frenchman, Buffardin.

Quantz later explained that the four months spent with Buffardin had been devoted entirely to the playing of swift florid music, because it was in such music that he had most to learn and Buffardin was so clearly superior. Thereafter it was as a flute player, and a composer striving to give the flute a really wide, representative repertoire, that Quantz was known. He went to Naples and overcame Alessandro Scarlatti's dislike of woodwind instruments (Scarlatti had been of the school of thought that dismissed the woodwinds for never being in tune). He went to Paris, where he found French orchestras unsatisfactory and the French habit of beating time by banging on the floor with a stick quite detestable. French flute players, however, continued to impress him. In 1727 he went to London and turned down invitations from Handel and others to stay, preferring to return to Dresden to play in the King of Saxony's orchestra.

Then came the royal tug-of-war. The Queen of Prussia wanted Quantz but the King of Saxony would not let him go. A compromise was reached. Quantz stayed in Dresden but was allowed to travel regularly to Berlin to give flute lessons to the Prussian Crown Prince, later to become Frederick the Great. When Frederick became king in 1740, he offered Quantz a salary which no sensible man could refuse and which the King of Saxony was not willing to match. In addition there were to be bonus payments: a fee for each composition, 100 ducats for each new flute he made. The partnership was launched.

Most of what Quantz wrote was intended for the flute, notably a series of some three hundred concertos (some for two flutes), 277 of which were preserved in Frederick's palace at Potsdam. They were played in numerical order, two per evening, at court concerts; the composer directing the orchestra and the king playing the solo part. Order of composition was strictly observed. If concertos Nos. 276 and 277 were performed on Tuesday night, on Wednesday the concert consisted of Nos. 1 and 2. Frederick's pride in his ability to play long slow melodies left its mark on these works, in addition to which Quantz also turned out a large number of suites, sonatas and chamber works for his insatiable patron.

It seems that Quantz took to making flutes for the simple reason that good ones were hard to come by. He began the venture in 1739, a couple of years before giving in to the blandishments of Frederick the Great.

Always impeccably in tune himself, he made no improvements to the instrument which would ensure that lesser players would also be in tune. Seemingly he regarded the player's skill in compensating for the shortcomings of his instrument as a fact of life, an integral component of the art of playing, not to be remedied by technical means.

But pitch was something else again. The eighteenth century had no conception of such a thing as standard pitch. Even today pitch varies from one country to another, but two hundred years ago an instrument perfectly in tune in town A might be disastrously out of tune in town B, a dozen miles down the road. If a flute was in tune with other instruments, it was probably out of tune with the church organ, for church pitch was higher than the pitch accepted in halls and opera houses. Clearly it was necessary to have a flute capable of playing at whatever pitch was required, in ensemble with whatever other instruments it happened to encounter, and adapting itself to whatever temperature existed in a hall or theatre.

Flute makers before Quantz had tried to beat the problem. Their solution was to lengthen the tongue joints in the various parts of the flute, so that extra wooden rings could be inserted between sections in order to lower the instrument's pitch. The trouble was that the pitch was lowered unequally. As wooden rings were fitted, the right hand finger holes moved increasingly out of tune with those of the left hand.

Highly experienced, widely travelled and a perfectionist, Quantz decided that something more effective had to be done about this troublesome, unpredictable pitch. What he came up with was the running slide. By lengthening the pin of the pin-and-socket joint between the head of the flute and the first section of its body, he made it possible to lower pitch by as much as a quarter of a tone. This did not solve everything, however. With the pin lengthened to its full extent, the second and third octaves fell in pitch further than the first. Quantz knew very well that if one part of the flute was lengthened, the other parts should be adjusted in proportion, but still he relied on the player's management of embouchure and fingering to make good this remaining little awkwardness.

Theoretically, of course, the position of the stopper (the plug that closes the bore at the top end) should be different for every note of the scale. Flute players had long known that if the stopper were placed too far from the mouth hole, the second octave would sound flat and the third would become impossible, while the lower notes of the first octave gained in definition and power. Conversely, a stopper too near to the mouth hole sharpened the second octave, made the third octave easier to play though still sharp, and weakened the low notes. The stopper's position had to be a compromise, and trial and error had demonstrated that the best results were achieved when the distance between it and the mouth hole was equal to its diameter.

That was before Quantz's new invention. If a tuning slide were to lower the pitch of the flute, the stopper could compensate, so long as any adjustment to its position was minute. Quantz therefore set the stopper on a screw which could be turned from the closed end of the flute to make the kind of minimal, precise adjustment which would allow for the use of the tuning slide.

So far, so much better than anything that had gone before. At the same time Quantz turned his powerful attention to the shape and size of the mouth and finger holes. Originally mouth holes were circular, and so they remained, though decreasingly, well into the nineteenth century. But elliptical mouth holes began to appear alongside the originals in the eighteenth. According to the authorities, Quantz's mouth holes, which were of the new-fangled elliptical variety, measured 0.5 inch in length and 0.42 inch in width.

Quantz's third innovation was a key to discriminate between D# and E♭, less important for its pitch than for the fact that it improved other notes – all the sharps in the first octave and G# in the second. Quantz wrote a text-book, which goes by the snappy title of *Versuch einer Anweisung die Flöte traversiere zu spielen*, not only dealing with every aspect of flute playing as the eighteenth century knew it, but also finding space and time for a lively account of the music of the day. In this he explains how doubtful notes can be improved by half-opening or half-closing certain finger holes, and how, by turning the instrument inwards or outwards, the player can affect the intonation and vary the tone. The essential thing, he adds, is a highly developed sense of pitch, and to gain this a player should learn to make, or at least to tune, a flute for himself. I know a few players who subscribe to this philosophy and have built their own flutes.

Additional keys

It may have been the development of a bass flute in 1751 that suggested how further improvements to the normal concert flute might be brought about. Apparently a French invention, the bass flute was described in Volume VI of the *Encyclopédie* of Diderot and d'Alembert.

By this time extra finger holes permitted the standard flute to descend to C. The new bass flute was tuned in G, a fifth lower than the standard flute, and the extra length of tube demanded by this lower pitch led to the next technical advance in flute building: it made the use of keys essential.

The head of the flute described in the *Encyclopédie* is in two sections. From the mouth hole the windway passes into a brass 'elbow' which turns it back parallel to the mouth hole section and connects with the body of the flute. The first section of the flute supports the first three finger holes; the right hand finger holes are in the body's second section, and in the foot there is a hole for the F#.

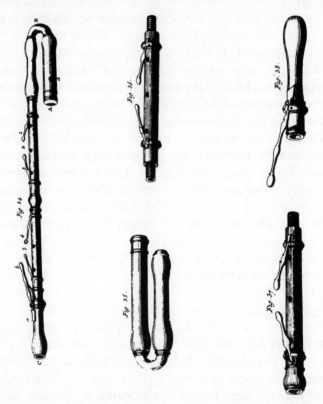

Illustration from Diderot's *Encyclopédie*, showing bass flute – apparently a French invention

These holes are too far apart and spread along too great a length to coincide even loosely with the fall of the fingers of the average hand, so keys were added, five of them altogether. The B hole and the E hole are left for the fingers, and keys take care of the other holes, including the one which operated the distant F# at the foot of the instrument, the equivalent of the C# key on the standard flute. But whereas the C# key had to be pressed to open the hole, on the bass flute it was the other way round: the key held the hole open on its spring, and it was closed only when the key was depressed. The key levers lay along the length of the instrument, turned to be conveniently placed for fingers necessarily anchored to the B and E holes. Given two and a half octaves from G a fifth below the standard flute, the term 'bass flute' is a misnomer. It was really an alto flute, and it is as an alto flute that we generally know it today, though you will still come across references to the 'G bass flute', so called to distinguish it from the deeper bass flute in C.

Round about 1770 attention turned to the possibility of a standard flute bored to provide a complete chromatic scale without the awkwardness of cross-fingering, a technique which left many notes sounding uncertain. Holes were bored between E and F# to give an F♮; between G and A to give a tempered G#/A♭; and between A and B to give an A#/B♭. With all these new notes came new keys. The one note of the scale which still required cross-fingering was C♮.

Keys and their levers solved some things, but they also created new problems. The capping of the holes had to be airtight or intonation suffered, and airtight keys continued to baffle flute makers until the 1840s. They baffled other instrument makers as well, for all woodwind instruments were developing along similar lines. Another difficulty was the mounting of the keys and levers on the body of the flute. The mounts tended to work loose and lose their immediate responsiveness to the fingers. First-rate players may well have decided rather to bear the ills they had on the unreformed flute than to risk the perils of the new technology.

However that may be, it was to be foreseen that the missing note hole for C should eventually be supplied. The supplier was Johann Georg Tromlitz, who lived from about 1730 to 1805, a flute maker and player from Leipzig who was well known as a soloist although he seems never to have held any important orchestral post. In addition to making a note hole for C♮, Tromlitz began to rationalize the position of keys and their levers, which had come clustering on to the instrument somewhat haphazardly. There was just too much work for the normal allowance of fingers to do. Sometimes the same finger had to stop a hole and press a key at the same time. It was common for the left thumb to have to work two keys. Another key, to be operated by the right thumb, made the instrument difficult to hold steady. Tromlitz designed keys which could be used by either of two fingers in situations where one of them was wanted elsewhere.

Tromlitz retired from the concert platform when he was sixty and devoted the rest of his life to improving his instrument. He left the flute with eight keys and the traditional six finger holes, with a more staightforward system of fingering, able to play in any key. To all intents and purposes, the flute seemed complete, but it had become a more complicated instrument than the one Frederick the Great played under the guidance of Quantz.

In fact the flute was still a long way from perfection. Faults of intonation were still built into it and had to be corrected by the player's skill. In spite of Tromlitz's hard work, too much was often demanded of the limited number of fingers of the human hand. And speed and agility on the eight-keyed flute proved beyond the scope of all but good players. After Tromlitz other inventors refined upon his refinements and improved his improvements, but it remained tinkering until Theobald Boehm found a mathematical solution to the problem in the 1830s.

The repertoire

In spite of all the technical progress made, the general standard of flute playing remained pretty low, perhaps because by now every second person of substance had taken to amateur tootling on the instrument. Take the Gentlemen's Concert, for example. This was a music club in Manchester in the 1740s, at which local amateurs met regularly to play together until Jacobites infiltrated it as a cover for their plots in 1745. The harsh breath of political subversion, not to mention the defeat of the Jacobites, shrivelled the music makers, and it was not until 1770 that a new generation tried to re-establish past enjoyments by setting up the Gentlemen's Concerts (in the plural this time round). But some years had to pass before the concerts really got going because the first twenty-four hopeful members were, to the last gentleman, flute players!

The great Quantz was partly responsible for this demographic explosion, because he improved the flute but also because he gave it so much music to play. He was not alone. As earlier in France, the improving performance of the professionals prompted composers to turn their attention to flutes as they had not done before. They wrote for it as a solo instrument and as an orchestral instrument, with the soloist having a slight edge to begin with.

Bach was a notable pioneer. As we have seen, he scored for the recorder in two of the Brandenburg Concertos, but in the Fifth of them it was the flute he explicitly required. Moreover he gave us the *B Minor Suite* for flute and strings and several sonatas with continuo as well as the A minor Partita for unaccompanied flute. It seems that, early on, such flute players as he had access to could not be trusted with major works, but somewhere along the line he got the services of one or two good ones. The *B Minor Suite* is so taxing that it remains difficult even for a player with a dependable modern flute at his disposal.

Handel wrote for the flute. Vivaldi contributed six published concertos and sixteen unpublished, as well as a number of sonatas. Moving on in time both Haydn (whose Sonata, arranged from a quartet, was written for the six-keyed flute) and Mozart added to its repertoire, to say nothing of a multitude of works by lesser composers and the excellent Quantz's three hundred concertos.

In 1778 Mozart visited Mannheim and Paris in search of a worthwhile appointment. The Mannheim orchestra was the first virtuoso ensemble in Europe and its principal flute was Johann Baptist Wendling, who had already toured

England and France with great success. Wendling seems to
have been the best flute player that Mozart had yet heard.

'He plays what is written in the score,' Mozart wrote
wonderingly to his father, 'and does not startle you by
playing something quite different.' In gratitude he included
Wendling's flute – along with oboe, bassoon and horn – in
the *Sinfonia Concertante* (K 297b). Other music Mozart
wrote for the flute included two concertos (K 313 and 314),
four *Quartets with Strings* (K 285, 285a, 285b and 298) and
the *Concerto for Flute and Harp* (K 299). In all these works
except the *Sinfonia Concertante*, Mozart was relying on
amateur flute players: the Duc de Guines in the *Flute and
Harp Concerto*, the Dutchman De Jean in the concertos
and quartets. But paid or not for their labours, they must
have had a way with a flute, for Mozart's music seems
intended to display the powers and personality of the
instrument itself, its agility, its ability to combine high
speed with easy natural grace, its lyrical expressiveness in
spinning out legato melodies such as these two from the
Flute Quartet in D Major:

By the late eighteenth century the flute was becoming a regular member of the orchestra, now taking its classical shape. But before, say, the 1780s, it was only an occasional sharer in the action.

Of the five symphonies which Haydn wrote before he became Assistant Kapellmeister to Prince Esterhazy in 1761, only one calls for a flute. Thereafter employment opportunities briefly improve. The first Esterhazy symphony (*Symphony No. 6*) requires a flute, *Symphony No. 7* two flutes, *Symphony No. 8* one. And in all three of these works, the flute is given expressive, characteristic music. For some reason Haydn didn't keep up the good work. Between 1762 and 1774 he knocked off forty-four symphonies, scoring in a flute in only seven of them. Some amends were made in *Symphony No. 54* which asks for two. Then, after 1780, every one of his remaining symphonies needs at least one flute.

It is the stormier, more intensely emotional, works of the middle of his career that tend to neglect the instrument, and even in the later symphonies the flute has little to contribute to stormy passages, but is reserved for moments of charm and emotional relaxation. The slow movement which gives the *Clock Symphony* (No. 101) its name passes through a storm, registering at least a few degrees on the Richter Scale, in which the key, G major, sinks into the minor. But calm and G major are restored by two flutes, two bassoons and the first violins, with interjections from the oboe, in music that can only be called enchanting:

The Flute

From the Andante, Haydn's Symphony No. 101

Like the later Haydn, Mozart often scored for two flutes
– as in most of the symphonies written before 1781 for
performance in Salzburg. This doubling up was simply a
way of ensuring that the flute would not be drowned by
the rest of the woodwind in a *forte* passage. But as a rule
Mozart relied on the oboe, with its then more reliable
intonation, for the treble voice in the woodwind section.
In the great $E\flat$ *Symphony* (No. 39), the flute is often no
more than a fleck of colour in a quiet passage:

The *Paris Symphony* (No. 31), written in 1778 to dazzle an
aristocratic French audience, and therefore deliberately
brilliant, uses two flutes. However the *Linz Symphony*
(No. 36) discards flutes altogether, and the three final
masterpieces, the *$E\flat$*, *G minor* and *Jupiter Symphonies*,
ask for only one.

In Mozart's operas there are innumerable passages in which the flute is exploited with great subtlety to contribute to, or comment on, the drama. But for all his appreciation of the instrument's potential, Mozart still overlooked it on occasion: maybe some of the orchestras he wrote for simply didn't have flute players.

Beethoven, in contrast, regarded flutes as indispensable in an orchestra – and not only in the orchestra. Among his earliest works, written in Bonn in his teens, is a *Serenade* scored for flute, violin and viola. This work, which is of greater interest as a juvenile work by Ludwig van Beethoven than for its actual quality, was probably composed in 1797 although it was published, as *op.* 25, only in 1802. That same year there appeared a version of the *Piano Sonata Op. 31, No. 3* for flute, violin, two violas and cello, which was published in 1810. The arrangement may not have been made by Beethoven himself, but if it was, it seems likely that he numbered an accomplished flute player among his friends and patrons in Bonn.

Flutes were included in the early dance music composed before he left Bonn, and two sets of minuets and German dances, dating from 1795, call for piccolos. All the symphonies demand two flutes, and in addition the *Fifth, Sixth* and *Ninth* demand a piccolo. His fondness for the piccolo is perhaps explained by his increasing deafness: the piccolo is included in a great deal of his orchestral music from 1805 onwards. It is not used merely to double the flutes, but to add effects of its own. The *Pastoral Symphony*, finished in 1808, has a sizzling lightning flash at the climax of the storm in the fourth movement which could be conveyed by nothing but the piccolo. The *Egmont Overture*, two years later, ends like the *Fifth Symphony* with a triumphant declamation. The exultation seems to drive its way upward through the score to burst out of the piccolos at the highest level of pitch the orchestra can reach.

What Beethoven did for the flute was not undone thereafter. Flutes have never fallen out of orchestral fashion since.

Four
The Modern Flute

'This instrument,' wrote Berlioz in 1843, in his *Traité de l'instrumentation et d'orchestration modernes*, 'which for a long time remained imperfect in very many respects, is now – thanks to the skill of certain manufacturers, and to the system of fabrication pursued by Boehm according to the discovery of Gordon – as complete, as true and of as equal sonorousness as could be desired.'

It was a triumphant moment, and Berlioz did well to pay it so measured a compliment.

William Gordon

Since the days of Tromlitz and company, various efforts had been made to improve the eight-keyed flute, but the trouble was that nobody could actually conceive of an instrument which was both perfectly in tune and playable by a human being. If the finger holes were to be made in the positions dictated by the diatonic scale, the fingers would not be able to reach them. The conclusion drawn on all sides was that the instrument must necessarily remain imperfect, and the imperfections be compensated for by the player's skill – as had been done since time immemorial.

Actually the conclusion was not drawn *quite* on all sides. A flute player or maker here and there continued to worry at the problem of how to reconcile the irreconcilable, and in 1830 or thereabouts the answer was found. As with technological strides in other arts and crafts there was, and remains to this day, some dispute about who precisely was responsible. Berlioz, in the extract quoted above, shared out the honours, but posterity has decided that they belong largely to Theobald Boehm. The truth probably was that great minds made similar deductions at much the same moment in time.

The Gordon to whom Berlioz referred was William Gordon, a Swiss soldier of Scottish descent who was a notable amateur flute player when not serving in the Swiss Guard of Charles X of France. In 1830 the French, having caught the habit of hiring and firing monarchs, ousted Charles X in favour of King Louis-Philippe, and Gordon abandoned soldiering to go to London, where he got the instrument makers Rudall and Rose to fashion two flutes to his own design. The novelty was that each note hole was placed precisely where it should be, so that each note was in tune, and the instruments produced a perfect diatonic scale. Because the holes were no longer determined by the natural spread of the fingers, keys were essential. We know what a flute designed by Gordon looked like from a diagram illustrating the *Méthode* for flute players published by the French musician, Côche, in 1839. This instrument left two finger holes to be stopped by the fingers of the left hand, and three for the fingers of the right. The other holes – and there were twelve, to sound all the notes of the chromatic scale – depended on keys.

Diagram of a flute by Gordon, from Côche's *Méthode*

Gordon and Boehm met in London, in either 1830 or 1831, no doubt brought together by their common passion for inventing a better flute. It was this encounter which led some people to wonder whether Boehm's improvements were all his own work. His approach was thorough and scientific, and because he took the trouble to explain what he was doing, the Boehm flute came, slowly, in the course of time, to dominate the market. It caught on at first more in France and Britain than in his native Germany.

Theobald Boehm

Theobald Boehm (1794–1881) was the son of a Munich goldsmith. By the age of sixteen he was not only a professional orchestral player, but had started to experiment with making flutes in his father's workshop. Playing and making continued to go side by side. In 1818 he was appointed principal flute in the court orchestra; in 1828 he opened a flute factory. To what extent he discovered for himself such things as linings to joint sockets and the pins that slide into them, or a mouth hole made adjustable by a sliding gold plate, he did not say. Such improvements had occasionally been introduced before he got to work, but he often implied that they were his inventions. He then turned to the key mechanism, improving the old French method of mounting the keys on an axle that ran between a couple of pillars on the tube body, on either side of the hole.

Early Boehm 'Patent Flute'

It was armed with a flute of this kind that, already a noted soloist, he visited London. There, apart from meeting Gordon, he heard the playing of Charles Nicholson, principal flute at the Opera and regarded as the outstanding English performer of the day. Nicholson was noted especially for the strength of tone he produced from a conventional flute, chiefly by means of larger holes than were customary. Seeing Gordon's instruments and hearing Nicholson's performance persuaded Boehm to undertake a radical rethink.

His aim was to preserve the natural quality of the flute's tone, while improving the instrument's intonation, extending its compass and adding to its power. He achieved accurate intonation by dividing the tube according to the laws of acoustics, not to the span of the hand, and backed up his placing of the note holes with mathematical calculations. In 1843 Boehm brought out his 'Patent Flute', preserving five finger holes as Gordon's flute had done, but with a system of keys more easily manageable than any that had gone before. The keys' tendency to work loose was the greatest drawback of the 'Patent Flute'.

Later Boehm 'Patent Flute'

Boehm had not finished yet. In 1846, after further serious study of acoustics, he decided that a cylindrical flute would give better results than the conical instrument of tradition which he had copied in the past. This, along with his improved keys (made as ring-keys, by which a player's finger can close a ring when covering a hole while at the same time operating another key that covers a hole on a different part of the flute), his system of clutch keys (making it possible for one key to close a hole at a distance from it), and his acoustically accurate boring of note holes all added up to the final Boehm flute which, with occasional minor improvements, was eventually to become the generally accepted, more or less universally employed, instrument. The greatest immediate advance on Boehm's work

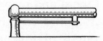

A needle spring

was the use of 'needle springs' with a rotary action, invented by his contemporary Auguste Buffet. Boehm's improvements were not confined to the keywork. In search of a more resonant tone he abandoned the conical bore found in flutes ever since Hotteterre-le-Romain (and still common in piccolos) and gave his instrument a cylindrical bore, while the bore of his head joint was made to narrow towards the stopper, first conically but finally in a parabolic curve. This is how flutes are built today.

Into the twentieth century

After Boehm's efforts, great players – or any players, for that matter – no longer had to struggle against their instruments' imperfections, as Hotteterre and Quantz and company had done so well. Learning to play was not as complicated and playing in tune did not require such skill. In theory that was the picture. In practice it was rather different. Too many flutemakers blithely ignored Boehm and his acoustical calculations, probably because they couldn't understand the mathematics. Intrinsically out-of-tune flutes went on being made, and indeed are still being made by the deepest-dyed reactionaries to this day. But quality tells. At the Great Exhibition in Paris in 1850 Boehm presented his treatise, with a flute made by his system. He got a prize for the flute, which was clearly superior to anything else available, and some people were impressed enough to read the treatise and discover that the sums were not as difficult as all that. Actually, according to mathematicians, the sums were ultimately found not to be exactly right either, but very nearly.

Now that the flute was capable of high technical performance, demanding music came along to suit.

In the interval the flute had consolidated its place in the orchestra, but had not gained much for solo performance. Weber wrote a *Romanza Siciliana* for flute and orchestra in 1806; Schubert composed his oddly neglected *Variations for Flute and Piano* on the song 'Trockne Blumen', from *Die Schöne Müllerin*, an imaginative piece of music with rich, profoundly moving harmonies, which turns into a show-display piece for the flute before it ends. There were one or two operatic opportunities, including the flute obbligato in 'Lo, here the gentle lark', by Sir Henry Rowley Bishop (composer also of 'Home Sweet Home'). In this a coloratura soprano and a flute in F flourish at each other at high speed, which sounds very exciting when well done, but must have set the teeth on edge with a less than excellent player on a pre-Boehm flute:

The Flute

(mount on) high

44

In 1835 came Donizetti's *Lucia di Lammermoor*, in which flute and doomed demented heroine warble together through the Mad Scene, and to which the same caveat about the quality of instrument and player applies.

However, since the creation of the Boehm flute, there was no reason except his own limitations why a player should not involve himself in the most elaborate scores, with their demand for flutter-tonguing and suchlike advanced techniques, designed to expand the flute's expressive vocabulary. This period gave flute players two of the most evocative pieces in the repertoire, both by Debussy: *L'Après-midi d'un faune* and *Syrinx*.

From *Prélude de l'Après-midi d'un faune*

from *Syrinx*

45

As flutes got better and music more demanding, the skill of flute players also scaled new heights. Famous names from the second half of the nineteenth century were those of the brothers Albert Franz and Karl Doppler, internationally celebrated soloists, successful composers of operas and ballets, and noted conductors. Meanwhile in Paris, Paul Taffanel was enjoying a similarly many-sided career, as soloist, conductor and teacher. Under the guidance of teachers of his calibre, France was regaining its pre-eminence as the home of the flute, a pre-eminence marvellously demonstrated in one of the most celebrated flute players, Marcel Moyse, who was born in 1889.

The name of Marcel Moyse will occur later in this book, in connection with recordings and, more especially, with his studies on sonority which no ambitious flute player can afford to ignore. But Moyse, though the most celebrated, was not the only distinguished French flute player who brought the art into the twentieth century. Another was Louis Fleury who, before his death in 1926, pioneered a new direction for flute music by turning to the past. His ambition was to get the flute's repertoire better known. At one end of the enterprise he used his reputation to introduce new works to audiences. At the other he dug up and restored to life the forgotten music of past centuries, forming the Société des Concerts d'Autrefois by way of framework. In so doing he set a trend.

The growing complexity of music during the nineteenth and twentieth centuries inevitably provoked a reaction in favour of a simpler age. Second only to the piano, the flute remained the favourite amateur instrument, but few amateurs were, or are, equipped to make their mark in music by Bartók, Stravinsky or Schoenberg. So, with all these amateurs around and nobody supplying their musical wants, there was a market for hearing as well as playing early music.

After the eighteenth century, the seventeenth was resurrected. Archaeology hasn't stopped there, but has continued digging further and further back in time until today the earliest written music, and specially built instruments to play it on, are commonly available.

The recorder's return

And what happened as a result of these antiquarian enthusiasms? The recorder was reborn, no less, and set about multiplying like a colony of rabbits. It has not joined the orchestra for the good reasons that prevented its joining in the first place. There the flute remains unchallenged. But outside the orchestra, after a couple of centuries of neglect, the recorder has made an astonishing comeback, and surely has a claim to be the most often attempted instrument. In fact, it is probably quite difficult to pass through the normal years of education at a normal English school and *not* make *some* noise on the recorder.

The man largely responsible for the recorder's revenge on history was Arnold Dolmetsch, a French-Swiss-Czech-German violinist who settled in England and became music master at Dulwich College before the First World War. Dolmetsch believed in making boys into practising musicians, and his determination to do so took him to the music of the past, and hence to old instruments. As early as 1890 he was making instruments regarded as archaic – clavichords, harpsichords and lutes. In 1925 he inaugurated the Haslemere Festival as a platform for these instruments as well as for the recorder. He set up a factory to manufacture recorders, in all the varieties needed for a consort, of course.

In the audience at the first Haslemere Festival were Max Seiffert, a Handel scholar, and Peter Harlan, a German guitarist and instrument maker, who took up manufacturing recorders more or less after Dolmetsch's pattern. Harlan and Seiffert carried the reborn recorder all over Germany, which, like England, found that no instrument was more accessible to the general run of children. Soon colleges of music found it necessary to teach the recorder to the would-be teachers, and so the movement gathered pace. To add to the excitement, composers began to regard the recorder with a friendly eye: Carl Orff in the 1930s included music for it in his *Schulwerke*; British composers such as Benjamin Britten, Lennox Berkeley, Malcolm Arnold and Edmund Rubbra later wrote adventurous and appealing stuff for the recorder which has no taint of antiquarian pastiche. Publishers did their bit, disinterring Telemann and his forerunners and bringing out reliable editions.

The revival of the recorder has given back the possibility of making music to many an amateur otherwise condemned to silence in an age of great orchestras and great solo artists. The recorder remains Everyman's instrument.

But your and my preoccupation must be with the flute. In this cause, let's complete our short survey of the history of the flute with grateful thanks to Albert Cooper, an Englishman who I believe has brought the flute near to perfection. Since Mr Cooper is prepared to give his own testimony, I shan't risk my own inadequate account of his achievements but thankfully allow him to explain for himself. So the next chapter is over to him.

Five
My Work on Flutes
by Albert Cooper

When I first started work at Rudall Carte and Co. Ltd. in
1938 the fashion in flutes was very different from what we
see today. Almost everyone preferred a wooden flute.
Nobody ever thought about trying to improve the intonation; it was never questioned. The player was told he had
a good instrument and it was up to him to play it. Nowadays
the player tells the maker what he thinks is wrong with his
instrument and demands that it be made to his require-
ments. Undoubtedly some players are better judges of
intonation than some makers. Since 1945 wooden flutes
have declined in popularity. They are still produced in
London but the majority of players prefer silver, gold or
other metal flutes.

I left Rudall Carte at the end of 1958 to set myself up as
a flute repairer but soon changed course and decided to
become a flutemaker. The difficulties of producing flutes
singlehanded soon became apparent, especially as I make
all my own components. The question of what sort of flute
to make soon arose. Should I copy an existing make, as
some others had done, or should I work out an original
pattern? Since I am not a flute player and advice from
players seemed to conflict, I decided to measure up as
many flutes of different makes as I could lay hands on.
During my time at Rudall Carte I had been engaged on
repairs at various times and had had many different makes
of flutes through my hands. I had not failed to notice that
a variety of different sized tone holes were in use and that
the positioning of the holes along the tube varied consider-

ably. In due course I made a collection of flute measurements. With all this data I was able to arrive at some definite conclusions that I had not thitherto realized. My early flutes were made to a pattern which I abandoned after using it for about ten instruments, based on logical reasoning from faults and virtues found on other flutes. I then changed to a mathematically calculated scale, which was slightly different, and I was soon convinced that it was better. After several years I again made certain slight alterations, and I now feel that I have more or less reached the end of the road scalewise.

I like to think that I am a good listener. I do not mean that I have a good ear for pitch but that I like to hear constructive comments from players. The London players have become to me the most critical in the world and I believe that I have helped to make them so. We may not always be in full agreement but I hope the majority are on my side. One sometimes hears an interesting opinion from an amateur player; amateurs are by no means to be ignored, nor indeed are students. I feel it would be wrong if I were to learn the art of flute playing and inflict my ideas on my would-be customers. I can always get a good cross-section of opinion just for the asking, and that is more valuable to me than the opinion of one man, whoever he is. To satisfy the majority is the best aim, since no one can satisfy all.

The equal-size hole flute

Should there be any doubt, let us confirm the basic principles of tuning. If a hole is made larger it sharpens, and if made smaller it flattens. If moved towards the embouchure it sharpens; towards the foot joint, and it flattens.

For the purposes of this discussion my use of note names is based on the following conventions:

The first thing to establish for any flute is the octave length – the actual distance between the C2 thumb hole and the low C1 hole on a B foot joint, measured from the hole centres. Basic calculations to determine their relative positions assume a flute with equal-sized holes; I find it best to base the scale on the largest hole desired on the instrument. In any case, to arrive at a measurement for the octave length one must have two C holes of equal diameter, whatever size is used. It is not possible to measure an octave length between holes of different sizes.

The position of the A hole within the octave length is most important. Obviously the interval between C2 and A1, and between A1 and C1, must be exact. These intervals were arrived at by trial and error over a period of years. It must be remembered that the A hole is never in the wrong position, since A is the note the orchestra tunes to, and if the flute's A is out of tune it must be corrected by adjusting the head joint. To arrive at the positions for the rest of the scale a mathematical calculation is used. We now have to divide the interval C2 to A1 into three parts so as to get the positions for the B and A# holes, and the A1 to C1 interval into nine parts for the G# to C# holes. To do this, the distances from one note to the next for the semitones from A1 up to C2 must decrease by 17.835 per cent, and from A1 down to C1 it must increase by 17.835 per cent. Note that I work from the A hole in each direction: one cannot rely entirely on a constant progression throughout the scale length, as the 'chimneys' on the tone-holes cause varying degrees of flatness. An answer to this would be curved tone-holes without 'chimneys', but no means has yet been found of making the pads for such holes airtight.

I read this figure of 17.835 in a book on guitar-making, where it was given for working out the position of the frets on the neck. Boehm's schema was also based on string lengths, although I do not know if his string lengths were the same as mine.

I did make an equal-size hole flute based on Boehm's schema, but it was rejected. However, there is no doubt that Boehm's work was the greatest advance ever made for the flute. This should never be forgotten.

To get the best overall tuning compromise certain holes must for various reasons be moved from the position arrived at by mathematical reasoning. These include the F# hole, sharpened to allow for the flattening effect of the E and F holes, the low D1 hole, flattened to lower middle D2, which is slightly sharpened by the need to open the small C# 2 hole, and the C# 1 hole on the foot joint, which is flattened to help blend in the evenness of the chromatic scale and deceive the ear.

My graph and the covered-hole flute

The measurements I have discussed so far concern a covered hole flute with the same large-size holes throughout. But nobody would want a flute with large-size holes throughout the octave length; this may give a powerful low and middle register but one would run into difficulties with the top octave. We must therefore reduce the hole diameters to give the flute a better balance between all three octaves – most flutemakers use three or four diameters within the octave length.

A graph which I have worked out and refined over the years gives the distance that a hole must be moved when the diameter is reduced without altering the pitch of the note, but is of highly technical interest and does not belong in a book such as this. I have used this graph for many years and have found it accurate – it was arrived at by logical reasoning, taking measurements from existing flutes at the points where hole diameters change.

The open-hole flute

Open-hole flute measurements are not the same as covered-hole measurements – at least, I do not think they should be. On my flutes I have made adjustments to allow for the extra venting from the open-hole cups.

If you open up the key rise on an open-hole flute, what happens? As far as the low and middle octaves are concerned, everything except the lowest note on the instrument will sharpen slightly according to the extent of the operation and depending on what the key rise was in the first place. The notes that have a covered-hole key are more prone to pitch change than the notes that have an open hole key; the extra venting of an open-hole key in the first place makes it less prone to pitch change. If I am right about this, the key rise of an open-hole flute must be established before the instrument is designed, and – once decided on – not altered by any appreciable amount.

The pad washer screw on the covered-hole keys can also affect the pitch relationship with the open-hole keys. If the screw head is too thick it can have a flattening influence, in which case the key rise must be opened or the screw head reduced. In my view the type of pad washer used by Louis Lot is best, though I know that these old screw-on washers are not popular with today's flutemakers and repairers and I am probably the only one still using them. Apart from the very slight venting advantage they offer, I like to be able to adjust the height of a washer in relation to the pad level; with the other types the washer height cannot be altered once the screw is tightened. I should have thought that the washer height could affect the pitch of a note; consequently the correct relationship between open and covered keys cannot be overstressed.

A flute player once said to me: 'Why make the measurements different on open-hole flutes and covered ones?' He demonstrated on an open-hole flute by playing a few low notes and then compared the pitch of those notes by sealing off the open-hole key concerned with his finger without closing it. As he played, neither he nor I could hear any difference in pitch change; but this is no test. You must put corks or plugs in the open-hole keys exactly down to pad level to make a fair comparison. What the experiment does reveal is how very little air, if any at all, does pass through the open-hole key. It seems to me that the hole area is just a space for air to circulate rather than escape; this hole area in the centre of the pad undoubtedly has a sharpening effect and a slight correction in hole position in order to compensate is essential.

The head joint

The head joint is of course of paramount importance, not only for the sound it produces but also from the tuning angle. Most makes seem to conform within certain limits and, in London anyway, many flute players use a head joint that was not originally supplied with their instrument, often of a completely foreign make. This has always been so; it shows what enthusiasm some flute players have in their search for perfection. For some, life is one continual search for a head joint that has got a little something extra.

In my experience, most head joints suit my scales, some better than others and some, I have been told, better than my own.

It is hard to describe what I look for in a head joint; my ideas today are different from what they were last year, and no doubt they will be different again next year. Some head joints give a very slightly different width in certain parts of the octave, whether it be from low to middle or middle to top. Presumably there are various reasons for this – slightly different parabolic curves, varying embouchure sizes, angles, depths. I hesitate to be more precise than that.

No doubt my own parabolic curve can be improved, but I am satisfied; quite frankly I do not know how to improve it. Embouchure sizes, depths and angles offer much more scope to the researcher. In the past I was completely obsessed with tone holes, but now I have turned my thoughts more towards embouchures. Embouchure design has not changed much since Louis Lot's day, but it is possible that there is still something miraculous left to discover – time and further experiment will reveal this. One could safely say that embouchures have been made deeper over recent years – I have certainly joined that band-wagon. A few years ago the holes tended to get a little larger, but recently I have been guided in the opposite direction.

Since I am not myself a flute player, cutting embouchures presents quite a problem: I never try them as I cut them up to size by hand, and I fear much is lost here.

They say there is a world shortage of silver flutes, but there seem to be plenty of head joints around for investigation, and no lack of help and opinions from players willing to co-operate. The problem is to find time to analyse all the comments.

One thing of interest that did come to light recently regarding lip-plates was the angle of the overhang, the part immediately in front of the blowing edge. Flute players have been bending it up (and down) for years, and a varied collection of ideas has been expressed as to what this does, the latest being that if it is bent down more than normal it very slightly narrows the octave between the low and middle and in general improves the tuning between all octaves. This is only part of the octave problem and I think must be taken into account when investigating the parabolic curve in future attempts to improve the octaves.

Some flute players undoubtedly blow differently from others and need to adjust their head joints accordingly by pulling out or pushing in to arrive at the same A. Also, with different sizes and depths of embouchure holes no definite measurements can be given from the centre of the embouchure to the centre of the A hole. As a rough guide, as near as the eyesight will allow, when you push in a head joint 1 mm you sharpen the pitch by one cycle per second, so by pushing in 5 mm you would sharpen your A440 to A445.

Conclusions

I have often been asked what sort of flute I think is best. I should choose a covered hole model with offset G and A keys and a split E mechanism; this is best for me but I readily accept that it is not the choice of the majority. An open hole flute with G and A keys in line just does not suit my left hand – I find it uncomfortable to hold and if playing should not feel at all relaxed, which is essential for a good performance. Not that I am in any way against the open hole flute – if I had to perform modern music which required quarter tones and glissandos that only the open hole flute can offer then I should use one, provided it had offset G and A keys and a split E mechanism. I would want flute playing made as easy as possible.

I have heard from several sources that my scales have been tested by various electronic means. Although I have never done this myself, these tests have influenced me up to a point by confirming some tuning problems and guiding me in which direction to move. I think it would be a mistake to tune the fundamental notes of the low octave by electronic means, as the notes that need corrections or compromises would be forgotten; one must know where the compromises are necessary. The ear of the player is the ultimate test as far as I am concerned.

I have always thought that the covered-hole flute was better in tune than the open-hole flute. The open-hole flute probably has the best middle octave and I accept that on this account the open-hole flute player is prepared to accept minor tuning faults. I think you could increase the five hole diameters and you would get the same effect, although five larger than average cups would be required and the flute would look odd. I also think you could reduce the five open-hole diameters; that would give the same venting as the covered-hole flute, but I cannot see it being accepted. To get the best from each model I have always thought a flute with covered holes on the left hand and open holes on the right hand was the best compromise, and I am surprised there are not more of these flutes around.

A common tuning complaint is sharpness on the head joint side of the A hole in both low and middle octaves.

Some flute players think they have a sharper pitched flute because of this, when in fact the opposite is the case. The flute plays sharp because it is made too flat. This sounds like a contradiction: but if your A is right (and it always is, because you tune to it by adjusting the head joint) the holes of the notes that are sharp must be moved away from the embouchure, which shortens the octave length, thereby sharpening the scale so that the offending notes will be flatter.

The question of which metal gives the best tone seems to me unanswerable. I have made head joints of silver, gold, stainless steel, pewter and even one that was half silver, half gold, and I am still none the wiser. I was attracted to stainless steel by its appearance and hardness, to pewter because of its softness and the fact that it is used extensively for organ pipes, for which it is particularly suited. I am told that it is best that organ pipes have a seam and as seamless pewter tubing is not available my head joint also had a seam. I cannot describe the difficulties of soft soldering a pewter embouchure chimney to a pewter lip plate and then in turn soft soldering it to a pewter tube with a soft soldered seam without the whole thing melting.

My present researches are directed towards perfecting the head joint. Nothing stays the same and I am constantly trying to improve things in a never-ending effort to make flutes sound even better.

Albert Cooper, London, 1982

Six

Maintaining a Flute

As you may suppose, I am the proud owner of a Cooper flute or two and, being so lucky, I try to deserve my good fortune by looking after them properly. Various physical hazards threaten the flute: dust, sweat, extremes of temperature, generalized assault and battery, but the biggest threat of all is the owner who does not care. Yet maintaining the flute demands neither hard labour nor – unless you go in for home repairs – skill. All it amounts to is a few simple commonsense routines.

Clean and safe

First, keep the instrument clean. After each practice or performance, wipe the fingerprints off it, using a soft cloth moistened with alcohol or something of the sort and not on any account with Brasso. This counsel is directed, of course, to owners of metal flutes and more particularly silver ones, on which sweaty fingerprints, if neglected, will turn black. To me, a dirty instrument suggests a sloppy performance all round. How can a player with so little fondness for his flute expect to play it well?

Everyday maintenance is largely a question of ensuring the flute's safety when it is not in use. You don't leave it lying around in the dust, you put it in its box. Furthermore, you make sure the box is stored in a safe place so that an incautious elbow will not send it crashing to the floor and it is protected against either too much heat or too much cold.

Handling

Before it reaches this safe housing it has to be taken apart and this can be a damaging operation if done clumsily. When detaching the head joint from the middle, take care not to grip the lip plate or the keys. The lip plate bends easily, and since the manufacturers have gone to some trouble to get it at the right angle for blowing, it is a pity to waste their efforts by wrenching it out of true. Similarly the keys are delicate pieces of machinery whose precision is essential for good playing. They are not to be used as levers for forcing the joints apart. The left hand should hold the head joint just underneath the lip plate, while the right hand holds the middle joint by the barrel. In the same way, when you take off the foot joint the left hand holds the barrel while the thumb of the right hand holds down the bottom two keys, C and C #.

Follow these simple instructions and hopefully you won't get any bent keys. I am sure I do not need to point out that the instructions apply equally to putting the flute together as to taking it to pieces at the end of the day.

The case

The best insurance policy for the flute is a good case, in which the three joints nestle down snug as so many bugs in a rug. Some cases are so ill adapted to their purpose that when given a shake they sound as if there is a whole bunch of knives and forks inside. My own cases are specially made in New York, each out of a single piece of wood and lined with what I take to be velvet. They are designed so accurately that you could shake them from here to kingdom come and all you would hear is silence. Not everybody can go to the length of a custom-built case, I know, but it is important to contrive some means of keeping the flute immobile inside the case, for the more it rattles around the more it is likely to get out of adjustment. Some flute makers supply protectors, little rings that fit on to the end of the head and the bottom of the middle joint, in order to lessen the danger of shocks and blows to the precision tooling. This may be just the thing for kids who don't discriminate between their treatment of a flute and a cricket bat, but for those among us who have learned to tell the difference, and especially for professionals, I would discourage the use of protectors. If they are too tight a fit, they risk wearing out the very connecting pieces they are meant to be safeguarding.

Personally, I observe one further ritual in the safe bestowal of my flutes, which you may copy or reject with scorn as you wish. Off-duty flutes in my keeping are always left lying (in their cases) north to south. I do this for the good pragmatic reason that I find the flutes work better when aligned north-south than when left haphazardly around. I presume the scientific explanation lies in magnetism, a force which nobody knows too much about. Treating myself with the same consideration as I give a flute, I also arrange my bed north-south. I understand Charles Dickens thought of this before I did. Sometimes when he booked into a hotel the room practically required redecorating to get the writer and the magnetism in line.

Problems of temperature

There is often not a lot one can do about extremes of temperature, either in countries like Britain – where we are just getting into air-conditioning – or in countries like the United States which include a whole continent's worth of climatic variation. Touring the States you can, within the space of a week, take your flute south where it is seventy-eight degrees Fahrenheit all the year round (except when it's ninety-five), and take it north where it's twenty degrees under. This sort of treatment is the quick road to the repair shop, for flutes thrive best when they are kept at a constant temperature. One can only try to limit the harm when traversing continents. A thing I make sure of is never to deliver up my flute into the luggage hold of an aeroplane.

It really freezes up there and besides, airlines have been known to lose luggage before now.

The part of the flute which can be most damaged by extremes of temperature is the pads on the keys, which change shape if they are too warm or too cold. Extremes of dryness and humidity are a related threat to the pads, and of the two, dryness is the worse. It tends to shrink the pads so that they don't fit properly. Humidity will swell them a little bit and, with luck, swell them evenly to the improvement of the music and the relief of the player.

Repairs

However careful and considerate you are, you can't postpone for ever the moment when repair is needed. When this moment arrives, my own belief and practice is to trust to the expert and not meddle myself. For one thing, mending flutes takes a lot of time and I prefer to spend my time practising. For another, it takes a lot of skill, which I haven't got. You may be thinking it's all very well for me to talk; I have several flutes at my disposal and can retire one to the repairers for a period without noticing the loss. Very true. I understand very well that, when flutes are thinner on the ground, the temptation to make one's own adjustments is great, especially for the British among us. If ever there was a do-it-yourself nation, Britain is it. Some of my flute-playing colleagues not only do running repairs to their instruments but actually build them in the first place. This has paid off for flute players at large, in that Albert Cooper's improvements were made in close consultation with performing musicians who took an interest in the making of their own instruments. But all the same I counsel prudence to do-it-yourselfers, and in justification of my cautious attitude I would cite a little story, not from Britain but from Japan.

One day in Tokyo I visited the Muramatsu showrooms to take a look at all the flutes, flute records, and flute paraphernalia on display there. Among the gadgets was a very fancy up-to-the-minute screwdriver with half a dozen interchangeable heads to it. 'How's that for a screwdriver!' I exclaimed, all admiration. 'That,' said Mr Muramatsu, 'is not a screwdriver. It is a flute-wrecker. Every time I sell somebody one of these I can be sure to have his flute in next day to be fixed.' So you have been warned. A screwdriver (or a nailfile or a kitchen knife or any other piece of hardware you care to mention) in the wrong hands can be an offensive weapon occasioning actual bodily harm.

Part Two

Playing, Practising and Developing Technique

I take it you have decided to learn to play the instrument whose ancient history and modern perfections we have just briefly surveyed. As somebody who has trodden this path before you, I wish you the best of luck and will try in the following pages to map the way and straighten out misleading detours. You have made a three-sided commitment: to music, to developing your ability to communicate with other people, and to mastering the flute. These three things generally develop alongside each other, but from the point of view of your conscious effort the third comes first.

You are not just trying to play the flute with a certain amount of skill. No. Your ambition must be so to master the flute that it becomes a part of yourself: not just a metal tube that hard blowing and clever fingers can bring a tune out of, but an extension of the physical, mental and spiritual organism that is you, an extra limb which functions with (almost) the same unconscious ease as other parts of your body. Well, I shan't begin by deceiving you: it takes some years, like half a lifetime, to find it more natural to have a flute to your mouth than not, and it is not unknown for flute players to sit in orchestras to this day content just to be competent and get the intonation and tempo right. That's not a point of view that appeals to me. That's not the way to enjoy playing the flute, or – equally important – to play the flute so that other people enjoy hearing it. Remember, the listener is your target, whether you are just beginning or have already learnt a few tricks. Communication is the name of the game, and your ultimate goal – upon which a corner of your eye should be fixed throughout the succeeding pages – is to absorb the flute into your bones, muscles and nervous system.

But before we get down to this programme, let me make a general proviso. In what follows I have done my best to put my experience to use on your behalf, but I don't want you to regard what I say like the Ten Commandments or the First Law of Thermodynamics, to which the only proper response is submission and acceptance. Flute playing is a human activity, and there are no two human beings the same. It follows that not only your problems but your solutions to problems will be different. There is no off-the-peg generalization, such as the multiplication tables, which fits everybody. Therefore you have a responsibilty to discover, by trial and error, what suits you as an individual. On the other hand, in spite of all their differences, human beings are fashioned to a similar pattern, and this similarity does permit some cautious recommendations on the best way to go about things. So I urge you, while you are learning the flute, to do two things: one is to make your own discoveries, and the other is to be open to ideas different from your own. Be prepared at least to think about and try new ways.

Read this book in this spirit of openness and experiment. Even players who ultimately develop a completely individual method which suits nobody else in the whole wide world have to start somewhere. Treat my statements as a point from which to begin, and if it proves to be a point of departure, so be it.

For the moment, leaving individuality aside, let's begin at the beginning.

Seven
Physical Aspects

Standing

I like to stand while practising, for two reasons. One is that the chair designed for several hours' flute-playing at a stretch has yet to be made, existing chairs offering certain discomfort and likely deformity to conscientious musicians. The second reason is that practice is about performance, and since I must stand in a concert, it is sensible to get used to doing it. A generalization I am willing to risk is that practice should as far as possible reproduce the circumstances of performance. If you are required to stand for twenty minutes or a couple of hours – playing beautifully the while – your muscles have to be accustomed to it. It follows that orchestral players, who must sit out a concert, should sit to practise: I shall get round to their problems shortly. Meanwhile I suggest you stand.

How you stand is important, not only because you have a lot of standing to do in the coming weeks, months and years, but also because your stance affects your breathing, your control of the flute, and the freedom with which you play it. The object is to be stable, at ease, and balanced, and the first thing to make sure of is to get yourself firmly planted on the floor, neither stiffly to attention like a Guardsman, nor slouched like somebody at a bus stop with the cares of the world on their shoulders and the weekend shopping in their hands.

Starting at ground level, my first suggestion is that you wear comfortable shoes. This counsel is addressed particularly to girls, on whom fashion frequently imposes penitential footwear. I suggest you resist the demands of fashion in favour of the flute and your feet. For example, high heels distort the stance, and are therefore in my view to be avoided. However, in accordance with the precept that practice is for performance, if you intend to perform in unsuitable shoes, you should also wear them while practising. At the time of writing, even lads are liable to spend their days in high heels, but, come concert night, they must change into the flat-heeled shoes of formal dress, thus abruptly, at the moment of performance, making a new set of demands on their muscles.

Standing Position
Angle the music-stand slightly to your left

My own experience provides a cautionary tale on the need for practising in the sort of shoes in which you have to perform. Some time ago I was the victim of a rogue motorcyclist who left me in the ditch with a couple of broken legs. After surgery and so forth, I eventually got back on my legs, but with my feet not back to normal it seemed easier to practise without shoes. When it came to the first post-accident concert, I regretted it fast enough.

Not only were the unaccustomed shoes uncomfortable, but – moderate though the heels were – they threw me off the balance learned barefoot.

So, first point: comfortable shoes which can eventually appear in public. Next, how to stand easy. I won't lay down laws about this, but tell you what I do in the hope it proves useful. I like to stand with my feet slightly apart, the left pointing slightly left, the right pointing slightly right, at the angle of ten-to-two on the face of a clock, and with the right leg braced to carry my weight. My shoulders are not parallel with my hips but swivelled slightly round to the left. I judge the extent of this swivel by aligning the hole (in the head piece, through which I am about to blow) with my left foot. Then off I go.

Whatever the alignment of shoulders to hips and feet, it is important to stand upright. There are several good reasons for this. One is that an upright posture helps the balance of the body and therefore improves muscular control. Unless you can yet your muscles to obey your smallest whim, you won't make the music you intend. A second reason is that standing straight conserves energy. If you stoop forwards as you play, you oblige your leg muscles to waste energy by tensing to prevent your falling over altogether. And thirdly, you can't breathe properly unless you stand straight.

Breathing for flute playing is a different activity from the unobserved in-and-out of air which serves for ordinary purposes. Shortly I shall have further things to say about breathing, but for the moment it is enough to stress that a flute player must be able to use his breathing equipment to capacity. This is a requirement that we share with singers, and if you ever have a chance to see singers perform, you will notice that great voices don't go with rounded shoulders and a caved-in chest. Like a singer, you have to stand with your spine at stretch, so that you can lift your rib-cage, fill your lungs and open your throat. Then you can let fly – if the music indicates such a course of action. Breath is your raw material. You need lots of it.

Your lungs are your storage tanks, and they operate best when you stand up straight and give them a chance to expand.

So now you have your feet firmly on the ground and are breathing like a prima donna in training. I hope you are standing at ease. I personally am not a member of the flute-playing school which instructs students that their first and last duty is to relax, for on duty muscular control is necessary. But control doesn't mean you have to be rigid. In particular, the position of arms, hands, fingers and head must be flexible, as well as under control, because – breathing apart – the controlled flexibility of these parts of the body determines the sounds you make. So you have three things to aim at in standing up: stability, straightness and suppleness.

At this point, from long acquaintance with young flute players, I would like to utter a warning. Granted you must not be tense to the point of immobility, but in my experience immobility is not an affliction which students greatly suffer from. On the contrary. Only too often they sway in time with the music as if they thought themselves responsible for choreographing it as well as playing it. Presuming you have not yet caught the dancing disease, I shall try to immunize you against it, for it really is a bad habit which gets in the way of the music. For example, it is not unknown for a young player to sway to the left on a phrase and make a little jab in the air with the flute to nail down the beat, then sway to the right and repeat the performance. This way of keeping time puts the music in a straitjacket, which does nothing for its charm. Keep your metronome in your head or on the mantelpiece, not in your arms and legs. Moreover, exaggerated movement uses up the energy and the oxygen which should be spent on the music. Some (small) movements help you to get a note you are after, and such movements you may make with my goodwill, but all others are simply a waste of scarce resources. And the faster the music, the scarcer will be those resources, and the more spendthrift the over-lively musician who uses them up without having to.

Having told you what not to do in the way of ballet-dancing, I can now sum up the instructions on how to stand: put your feet on the ground, keep them there, stand up straight, be still, and concentrate on playing the flute.

Sitting

A problem for the standing flute player is the music-stand. Either he raises it high enough to look the score comfortably in the eye – in which case the audience is treated to the blank prospect of a music-book surmounting a pair of anonymous legs; or he lowers the stand sufficiently to see the audience over it – in which case he must bend unnaturally forwards to read the notes. The short answer to this dilemma is to memorize the music.

This is not a dilemma which confronts the player who must sit, but he too has his problems, more particularly when he is part of the woodwind line-up in a full symphony orchestra. The flute is the odd man out here because it is side-blown, amid a bevy of front-blown instruments (oboe, clarinet, bassoon). When standing, one can overcome this sideways bias by swinging round the shoulders in relation to the hips (as already described), which lessens the tension on the back muscles and permits painless performance at length. But sitting in the orchestra, in a rank of woodwind players, chairs aligned and music-stands parallel, is another thing entirely. Your front-blowing comrades directly face the score and the conductor. You are twisted in your seat and squinting at both, your own nose blocking out half the information you need. The result is cramp in the upper left arm, and it can't do the eyes any good either.

Rather late in life, unfortunately, I solved this problem for myself. Leaving the music-stand in line with all the others, I turned my chair slightly to the right, so that if the conductor was at twelve o'clock, my chair faced two o'clock. Thereafter the music and the conductor were comfortably in my line of vision and there were no more

Seated Position
Angle the music-stand slightly to your left

cramps or squints. The only drawback is that some members of the audience may conclude you are not on speaking terms with the first oboe. But the fact is that, thus adjusted, you give a better performance, and as long as the first oboe knows you are still speaking to him, that's all that matters.

If you must sit to perform, you must sit to practise, and given the general inadequacy of chairs, you have my sympathy. All I can urge is that you will survive better on an austere, traditional, kitchen-type chair than on anything which modern inspiration has designed for comfort. The real test is a Bruckner symphony. If you can outlive that sitting down, you have a good chair.

Breathing

This is a vital subject and more important for flute players than for most of the population, but I think it is made unnecessarily difficult by technical descriptions, especially by glib references to the diaphragm, which could be down

The Diaphragm
The position of the diaphragm
in relation to the large organs
of the chest

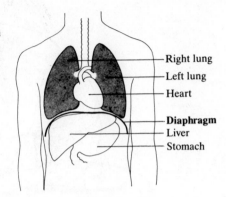

- Right lung
- Left lung
- Heart
- **Diaphragm**
- Liver
- Stomach

The Movement of the Diaphragm

 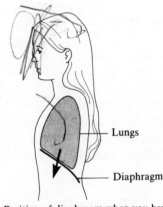

Lungs

Diaphragm

Position of diaphragm when you have
breathed out: relaxed diaphragm
moves up and is domed, lungs
deflated, chest cavity reduced

Position of diaphragm when you have
breathed in: contracted diaphragm
flattens and moves down, lungs
expanded, chest cavity expanded

the left side of his pants for all the average ten-year-old
knows to the contrary. For beginners, here are a couple of
experiments designed to show you which bits of your body
move when you breathe. You will need the help of your
dad, mum or best friend.

First, lie on your back on the floor, tuck your hands
under your waist a little, and get the person helping you to
put a hand firmly just above your waist, where the rib-cage
curves to right and left. Now take a deep slow breath. Note
that the expansion shifts the heavy hand pressing down on
you while at the same time your fingers can feel it at the
back. This is the diaphragm in operation.

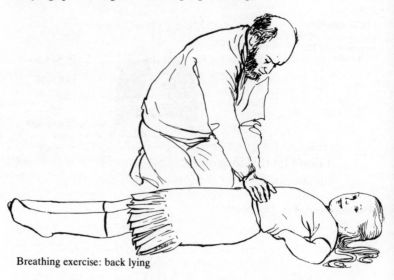

Breathing exercise: back lying

Next, still on the floor, roll over on to your front, your arms disposed alongside. This time your helper should put his hand at the top of your back at the level of the shoulderblades. Again a long slow breath. Again you will feel the expansion pressing against the restraining hand.

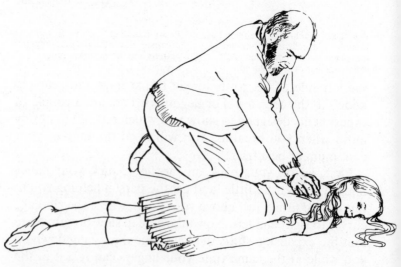

Breathing exercise: front lying

This experiment is intended to demonstrate that the lungs operate at the back as well as at the front, and much higher up the back than you may have supposed. In flute playing every last cubic centimetre of this capacity will be needed, so it's as well that you know of its existence and approximate location.

Breathing for an extra special purpose is not learnt in a day. It is something you have to spend a lot of time working on, but don't let this thought depress you. There is nothing superhuman about deep controlled breathing. Yogis do it, athletes do it, and you too can do it too – with a bit of determination and perseverance. Human beings are pretty similarly equipped for the purposes of breathing. One thing we all share is an ability to improve, so start the training programme immediately, and soon you will see the progress you have made – say, in a year or two or ten.

The training programme I have in mind is not daily work-outs in the gym or jogging round the park at dawn, but something much more specifically directed to flute-playing. In my youth, as a student in London, I used to practise holding my breath between one station and the next on the Underground. It was an interesting experiment which did me no lasting harm, but I don't suggest you follow my example, firstly because you may not have an underground railway to hand, and secondly because your anguished writhing might alarm the fellow passengers. But there are less public exercises you can try. They are designed to improve three things: the quantity of breath at your command, your control of it, and your economical use of it.

Stand with your hands either side of your waist, at the bottom of the rib-cage. Breathe in slowly while mentally counting one-two-three-four and note how the expansion of the ribs forces the hands out. Hold that breath to a count of four, then release it to a count of four. All the counting has to be done in the mind, because if you count aloud, you use up your breath for non-essential purposes. Do this at the start of practice each day. I suggest you

Breathing exercise: standing

begin with the easy target of four (in for four, hold for four, out for four) because I think even young children can accomplish this. After a couple of weeks stretch your ambition up to a count of five; then six; then seven; and so forth. But don't follow this advice too slavishly. Not everyone has the same capacity, and if you can begin the exercise higher up the sequence, so much the better. In that case decide for yourself the number you will aim at. Whatever it is, strive to increase it over the course of time.

Such exercises apart, here are some general tips on breathing. I have already spoken of the advantages of standing up straight, and I trust the lesson has not been ignored. So much for the physical organization.

The next tip is, remember you grow up. Small children cannot possibly breathe in the same way as professional flute players, so their understanding teachers tell them they can breathe here, there and everywhere throughout a tune, as well as in some other places in case of emergency. Very right and proper – for a beginner. But I have noted a tendency for the instructions of the first master to be observed long after they are no longer necessary. As you grow older and your lungs become more capacious, you must learn to cut down on all this panting. You will find the music soars as it never did hitherto, for each time you draw breath in mid-phrase you interrupt the music, you silence it, you catch it by the throat and stifle it – which is not what you intend, I hope.

So. Breathing is a big problem at the beginning, but patience, effort and the mere passage of time will reduce the dimensions of the problem. A further hint is that you should have an optimistic attitude. Human psychology works in an odd way, and if somebody *thinks* they can do something, they very likely *can* do it. This mind-over-matter effect certainly operates in the reverse direction: nothing is more calculated to put a block on your talents than the conviction that this particular problem is beyond you. So, be confident that your breath will last out to the end of the phrase, and when you find it does, you will have the assurance to do even better next time. The great thing is not to panic, because panic is bad for the nerves, besides using up breath drawn for other purposes.

Therefore you must practise taking a composed breath, even when time is short and the notes thick on the page. The composure of your breathing keeps your pulse-rate down and your breath in reserve for the music.

In my view there are three sorts of breath to master. First and basically, there is the deep breath taken before beginning to play or in any handy couple of bars' rest. I shall tell you what I do, in case it may be useful. I breathe in (composedly) to fill the lungs almost to capacity, then I pause just to make sure everything is in order and ready to go, and at the last moment I take a further snifter of air on top, so that with all that oxygen inside me I can really steam along.

That is my version of the flute player's super-breath. One needs a certain small amount of leisure to achieve it. But leisure is not always, nor yet often, guaranteed by the music, and frequently you must take a quick little breath to keep you afloat to the next point of full recovery. This is the second sort of breathing, what I call a 'bridge breath'. Because it is snatched at speed, it tends to be audible (for a soloist, that is: your breathing will not overly interfere

75

with orchestral performance). I tend to believe that audible breathing is a greater problem for women than for men, and attribute this to the higher pitch of their voices. Whether this theory is true or not, both men and women can learn to lessen the noise of breathing, and even get rid of it altogether. The secret lies in the relaxation of the muscles of the throat.

The third type of breath is also a survival technique, which it would be nice to be able to do without, but breathe we must, now and again, while we are blowing. Like the bridge breath, it has to be snatched at places where the music makes no provision for it, but it differs from the bridge breath in being even shorter, quicker and more covert. A good example is a series of repeated staccato notes. Insert a micro-breath into such a series and no one will be the wiser.

Such a technique demands experience, cunning and forethought. The path to mastery of it begins with breathing exercises, but also with considering the music you intend to play, to see *where* it offers a chance to breathe and *what depth* of breath each opportunity offers. But don't be too indulgent with yourself in this pre-planning. Too often young players at their last gasp will take a breath on the end of a phrase. if this is your experience, take yourself in hand and just chop out those unnecessary pauses. Remember, you need only one breath to survive!

Holding the flute

Theories (and disputes) on how to hold the flute date back as far as Johann Joachim Quantz, and very likely further. A couple of centuries later there is still not unanimity on the subject and I myself, during my years as a pupil, was given much conflicting advice. In the years since then I have reached a few conclusions. I trust they will not totally contradict what you learn elsewhere.

First, is there an ideal size of hand? Clearly not, but I think I am fortunate in having average-sized hands, neither clumsily large nor so small that the fingers don't fit comfortably on the keys. It is my opinion that people with small hands will do themselves a favour if they get a closed-hole rather than an open-hole flute. Blessed with regular-sized hands, I play an open-hole instrument.

Secondly, the whole problem of holding a flute boils down to one requirement: the need to keep it still while the fingers move. If the flute moves under the varying pressure of your fingers, the head piece bounces up and down, so that you blow over or under the hole as often as into it, with unfortunate consequences for the note, the tone and the overall impression.

To keep the flute steady I pinion it in a triangle of countervailing pressures. The three essential pressure points are: the side of the left forefinger, almost at its base; just below the lower lip, above where the chin juts out; and the tip of the right thumb. The left forefinger pushes the flute towards the embouchure, the chin is a stable point resisting this pressure, and the right thumb pushes in the opposite direction. And thus between thrust and counter-thrust, the flute stays still, whatever lively action is demanded of the fingers.

I shan't hide from you the fact that there are some people around who advocate the non-pressure system of flute-playing. Relax is their motto, and they propose as models for us all successful practitioners of relaxation such as a Mark Spitz or a Muhammad Ali. I remain unconvinced. I am sure Mark Spitz is totally relaxed when not actually swimming and Muhammad Ali when not actually punch-ing. For that matter I am moderately relaxed when not actually playing. But all physical activity involves the muscles to some extent and a relaxed muscle in action is about as much use as a broken spring.

So my advice is to put the pressure on – not too much, of course. I don't ask you to dislodge your teeth or dislocate your jaw. Just anchor the flute firmly between the three pressure points so that it remains steady, and get on with playing it.

Playing, practising and developing technique

The Three Pressure Points

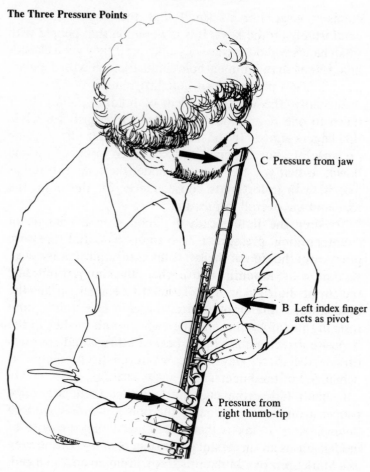

C Pressure from jaw

B Left index finger acts as pivot

A Pressure from right thumb-tip

Close-up of B

With all fingers off, the flute is rock-steady

My third piece of advice is to train the fingers to make as little movement as possible. This contributes to keeping the flute still. Slapping or hitting the keys too energetically makes the flute move in relation to the lips. It should remain absolutely constant, in the same place on the lips, no matter what you have to play.

To sum up: a firm hold and delicate fingering limit the accident area.

This becomes critical when the music is fast and difficult – the Ibert Concerto, for example, in which an unsteady flute ensures general and particular disaster. For beginners playing simple tunes it is not so critical; which is just as well, given the number and variety of technical problems which they have to tackle simultaneously. Even so, beginners should bear these points in mind. One thing the disputing authorities agree on about holding the flute (and I along with them) is the need for a balance between the right and left hands. In my view it is precisely the pressure of the hands (plus chin), previously described, which achieves the balance, thus creating a certain leverage which in turn leads to the flexibility of the fingers. So, even if you are still at the stage where the production of three intended notes in succession is a minor miracle, start to think about these ideas, experiment with them, work for a steady flute one day.

Playing, practising and developing technique

To help you on the way to this achievement, I suggest you start with the first exercise in Taffanel and Gaubert's *17 Daily Exercises*. This exercise was designed to improve the physical management of the flute. It is also a good idea to make your own experiments, improvising a tune of your own invention, and that way having fun while at the same time becoming familiar with holding and playing the flute.

That, in brief, is my flute-holding philosophy. I am aware I have put last things first and worked backwards, so now let me rectify matters and begin properly at the beginning, with the first grip on the flute.

Because each person has a different anatomy, I shall be very general about hand placements. Study the following drawings and try to use them as a basis for discovering the natural hand position for yourself.

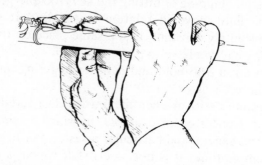

Front view of hands
Hands are relaxed; wrists drooped; fingers curved over the keys, lightly resting on or close to keys

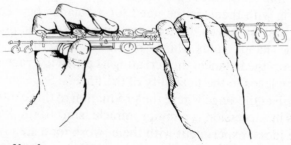

Back view of hands

Before you begin the experiment, a reminder: the natural position you are seeking is one which holds the flute firmly while allowing the fingers to move. True, at this point in time your fingers have about as much agility, independence and control of movement as a bunch of bananas, but future improvement starts here. From the beginning you must think in terms of (a) firmness and (b) flexibility.

Now look at pictures on p. 80. The left hand is in a position where it both supports the flute *and*, because it is steadied against the flute, provides a fixed point which allows it to act as a lever, giving strength to the fingers. To develop this hand position, first try it without the flute. Stretch your left arm forwards, holding it up in the air. Then relax the wrist joint so that your hand falls at the end of your extended arm. Look at your hand: it is in the same relaxed position as the hand of a baby sleeping in its cot. Now pick up your flute and simply bring your hand round the instrument by arching it slightly. Each finger should be poised in rounded position on each key. The little finger, while not in use, should be arched, but relaxed, not tense.

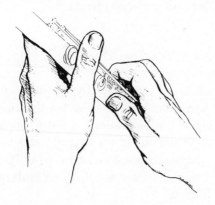

Thumb positions
Viewed from below: note that the left thumb's position on the key is straight, pointing upwards; the right thumb presses on the side of the flute

The thumb position of the left hand can be a problem for beginners. Commonly the trouble is caused by the thumb being placed too low on the B♭ key. I find it easiest to position the thumb between its tip and its joint – that is, at what should be the fleshiest part of the ball of the thumb. The drawing on p. 81 shows what I mean.

Naturally the exact placement of the hand varies with each player, but I hope my advice will be useful in helping you find the left hand position which best suits you, so that you can cope with the difficult technical problems that for sure lie ahead.

Next look back at the right hand position in the drawings on pp. 80–81. Try the same experiment. Stretch out your arm and relax your wrist, allowing the hand to droop naturally. Now, instead of curving your hand round the flute, as with the left hand, lightly place your relaxed fingers on the appropriate keys, maintaining the gently rounded position achieved in the experiment. Simply place your right hand straight on the flute, arching the fingers as naturally as possible.

At this point, with your fingers in position for take-off, it is time to check on overall leverage, that is, the three pressure points – left forefinger, chin, tip of right thumb. If all is in order you are ready to go.

Lips

But not quite yet, perhaps. There are the lips to be taken into account.

As you will learn very rapidly, if you don't know it already, the word wind players use for the shaping of the lips in playing is 'embouchure', a word taken from the French and none the worse for that in these days of racial equality and the Common Market. Certainly the English language has no substitute to offer, so embouchure it is, for you and for me.

In the whole of flute playing, there is scarcely anything more individual and less subject to generalization than the embouchure. We all have different physical attributes, and nowhere are the differences more different than in the subtleties of the mouth: the size of the mouth itself, the shape and thickness of the lips, how they come together when the mouth is closed, the space between them when it is open – all these are unique for each person. And that only refers to outward appearance. The inside of flute players' mouths, known only to God and their dentists, is a whole new world of possibilities and differences. If you were to run all these possibilities through a computer, you would come up with some surprising results, I think. Apparently similar embouchures can produce very different sounds, while very similar sounds have been known to issue from apparently different embouchures. The lesson is that human beings can outwit computers – so far.

To give you an example: I have always thought myself lucky to have lips which are not overly thick and a mouth which is not extravagantly large. Large mouths and thick lips must necessarily, it seemed to me, have extra difficulty in adjusting to, or focusing on, the hole in the head piece. However, to bring my complacent logic down in ruins, there exist many flute players – such as my friend, Hubert Laws, an Afro-American – whose lips are generously ample and whose performance is first-class. The only safe deduction is that there are as many embouchures to fit the flute as there are flute players.

For this reason, I don't approve of teachers who talk in absolutes on this matter; who say 'This is how it is done,' or perhaps 'This is how James Galway does it.' Such dogmatism is about as useful as a blanket instruction to drive on the left, neglecting the existence of separate lanes, motorways, foreign roads and so forth. As in driving, so in flute playing, the rules change to take account of circumstances.

A good teacher considers each student separately and objectively, and in the first instance as an individual mouth, assessing the size and shape of the lips and the muscular structure. Of course the teacher's past experience forms an immensely valuable basis, but this is the foundation only, upon which the student builds his own proper embouchure. Too many teachers try to make their students reflections of themselves. Too many students have to unlearn habits that in the first place did not suit them. The need to destroy before you can build again is a tragic obstacle to progress – tragic because it can so easily be avoided by sensitive teaching. So be sceptical and experimental in the matter of the embouchure.

Having warned you not to believe a word I say, I shall now proffer a thought or two on how to organize the embouchure.

Just as the hands should be balanced, so, in my view, there should be a balanced tension in both halves of the embouchure – that is, the upper and lower lips. This is what is called spreading the load, a useful stratagem on many occasions. For example, when carrying luggage, it is more comfortable to have equal burdens weighing one down to left and right than to hump a single outsize suitcase which has one staggering out of shape along the pavement. Similarly, things go better on the flute when the lips are under similar pressure.

Playing the flute Remember there are many different embouchures

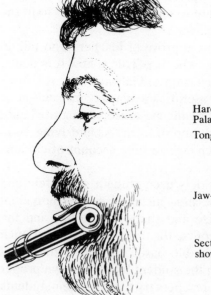

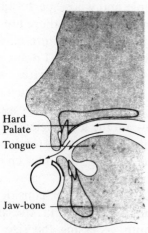

Hard Palate

Tongue

Jaw-bone

Section through the head and flute, showing path of the air-stream

An immediate qualification is needed. If the tension is equal, it is more equal for the lower lip. Both halves of the embouchure have to be taut, but the bottom lip, which slightly overlaps the hole, must be constant, while the top lip, manoeuvring the stream of the breath, has a small degree of flexibility – but I mean something minuscule, infinitesimal, totally unobservable to anybody else.

Presently I shall come back to these micro-movements of the lips. For the moment let's concentrate on the tension required for the embouchure.

The muscles which form the embouchure are the same ones we use to smile. To remind yourself of their location, try smiling with your mouth closed, and feel the stretching of the lower half of your face. You need not actually smile while playing, although that might not be a bad idea if it improved your spirits, but before you begin practising make the smiling experiment in order to familiarize yourself with the muscular control of the embouchure. In fact you could try out a few different expressions. The fixed smile was the prevailing fashion when I was a beginner myself, but somewhat later it occurred to me that the necessary tension of the lips could be achieved just as well by turning them grimly downwards as happily upwards. I used to practise this grimace on my way to college in a bus queue of city gents in St John's Wood, London, to their evident discomposure but I hope to my profit. It taught me that there is not one single facial stretch which alone can direct the stream of the breath through the embouchure into the flute. As I say, it depends on the shape of your face. So, in getting to know your face, try the fixed scowl as well as the fixed grin.

So what is the embouchure *for*? If you have got this far in the book, I hope this question is beneath you, but for anyone who has been skipping and happens to light on this paragraph, the answer follows. First, the embouchure channels the breath to the required location in the hole in the head piece. It thus ensures that some sort of sound is produced.

But secondly and thirdly it determines the quality of that sound. It corrects the pitch, if this is required, and it controls the tone. These refinements are further discussed in later chapters. Meanwhile, take my word for it that the embouchure is an essential part of your equipment, the training of which will last for the remainder of your flute-playing life.

Eight
The First Notes

Here is my first commandment for flute players: never play an ugly note. There really is no point in making a sound on the flute unless it is a nice one, and this is just as true for beginners as for the people who get paid to do it for the public. The quality of sound is frequently not stressed enough to beginners, because so many teachers accept any quality just as long as a sound comes out. But I believe that the beautiful sound is always there, and can be found, learnt, and maintained for future use, if teacher and student take care in developing the first note.

How to produce the first note

To start with, the beginner should experiment in making sounds with the headpiece only, to avoid having to manage the whole flute and think of half-a-dozen things at once. I believe this kind of 'isolation' for working on particular problems, and indeed for concentrating the mind in daily practice. We all need to worry as little as possible, so why not identify what needs improving, isolate it, and get down to making it better?

Back to the lonely headpiece. As a beginner, your first task is to test out your embouchure – the set of your lips and their placement on the lip-plate which feel easy for you and produce results. The headpiece should be placed in the centre of the lips and supported there – not pushed in but held steady. Study the drawing on p. 88 to see how the headpiece should be centred. We each have a different sense of where to blow but, wherever that may be,

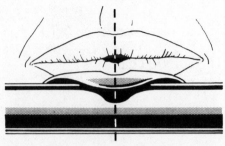

Centralize the lips so that the air-stream is aimed at the centre of the tone-producing edge of the blow-hole

remember to hold the headpiece firmly on the bottom lip.

It may take time to adjust your lips to the lip-plate. This is a common difficulty among beginners. Be patient and work on it.

Now form the embouchure. Stretch the lips so that they are in line or parallel with each other and touching each other, except for a very small pin-like hole in the middle.

Shaping of lip aperture

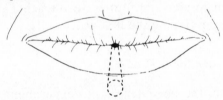

Pin-hole: be able to make the lip aperture minute and round, producing a rod-shaped air-stream

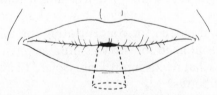

Wider slit: this produces a wide blade of air, which must – though – always be narrower than the flute blow-hole

Both lips share in operating the flute, so there should be a similar tension on them although, as I have said, the upper lip has to be a trifle more flexible than the lower. But neither lip should ever be seen to move. To the onlooker a flute player's mouth should seem as immobile as the Rock of Gibraltar.

Direction of air-stream
Be able to blow a narrow air-stream up and down your hand, using your lips to direct the angle

Using just the headpiece, blow through the tiny hole between your lips on to your free hand, to test whether the air column is flowing and channelled, or spread. You won't get very many notes until you have learned not to spread, but to channel.

Still with the headpiece only, start making sounds, going as low as you can at one extreme and as high as you can manage at the other. Be sure to make clear healthy sounds. Their quality should be open rather than small and closed.

When you have established the spot where you feel most comfortable when blowing, put the headpiece on to the body of the flute and try your first note.

Channel your air-stream

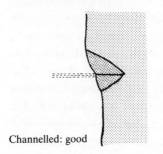

Channelled: good

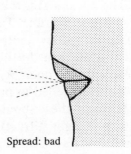

Spread: bad

There is great controversy about which is the 'best' note for a beginner to start with. I think it depends on the beginner, and a good teacher will instruct the individual in question to do what comes most naturally. The clues as to what is natural will have been provided by the exercises with the headpiece alone, clues which a sensitive teacher can pick up and advise accordingly. In general a note in the lower or middle octaves is the most easily accessible, but suit yourself, in the interests of a quick result, immediate encouragement and the production of a good sound rather than a poor one at the first attempt. The long haul starts here, so the launching may as well be splendid.

For demonstration purposes only, I suggest you take your first crack at a B♮:

All set and everything organized? Off you go then, loud, clear, round and steady, to a count of (say) five. Pause for breath and repeat. Keep this up for some time, holding on to your by now magnificent B♮ for as long as possible. If there is a teacher or someone handy, they can check on your stamina by counting aloud. Most of us find this a challenge and soon manage to play the next note longer than the one before.

Having played the first note and learned to hold it, really think and really listen. The sound should be centred, not too airy but full and very clear. An important factor in producing this desirable state of affairs is the inside of your mouth. The vocal and throat cavity should be as relaxed, open and free as possible. Take the flute from your mouth for a moment and try another silent exercise. Simulate a yawn, and while you do so, be conscious of that cavern measureless to man opening up in your throat. That is the sort of opening needed to produce a good sound. But not only that: your chest should be open too (you are still standing up straight, I trust). With throat and chest open, your whole body is a sounding board, assisting the flute.

The second note

Once a good clear sound has been achieved, it's time to pass on to the second note. The easiest plan is to go no more than a semitone away from your starting note, whether lower or higher. Again for demonstration purposes, I propose you move down from your B♮ to B♭.

When you can blow both B♭ and B♮ easily enough, compare them for evenness of sound. Your aim at the moment is to make them as similar as possible. The lesson on how to make them sound different comes later, but it begins here, because producing the sound you intend to produce is a matter of control. Your first lesson in control is playing these two notes with as nearly as possible the same quality of sound.

Alternate them a few times, making each a confident statement, holding them long enough to hear what is going on, and striving for a smooth transition between them.

Fitting notes together

Your next venture is to move from B♮ through B♭ to A, and so bit by bit to extend the boundaries of your exploration of the lower register. In this way, semitone by semitone, you add new notes and new fingers to your repertory.

With the basic pioneering done, the real complications begin. Fitting notes together combines several functions: control of the breath; use of the fingers; adjustment of the embouchure; and the constant vigilance of the ear, which must check that every note is in tune and the overall sound remains full and clear.

Putting technicalities aside for the moment, I strongly believe that the most important component of this operation is the sequence of sounds you imagine, the sounds you

Playing, practising and developing technique

Fingering Chart

(Black keys: closed. White keys: open. Shaded keys: optional – open or closed)

92

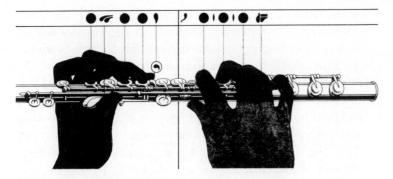

The Relation of the Fingering Chart to the Flute and Fingers
The flute shown has a B foot joint (with an extra key which enables you to play low B below middle C)

hear in your mind's ear, before you ever play them. If your mind is on target, there is every chance that other parts of you will find ways of rising to the occasion.

Other parts of the anatomy are involved, however, so let's briefly recapitulate on their organization. The first thing to make sure of is that the flute is held steadily between the three pressure points previously described. Second, be calm and breathe composedly, as also advised in earlier pages. Third, don't let that embouchure relax. And then – while keeping your ear stretched as overall quality-control supervisor – you can focus on your fingers. Be patient with your fingers, but firm, like the better type of Victorian parent. Playing a musical instrument is outside the normal experience of the average hand, so it takes time for the fingers to develop the strength, independence and agility now required of them.

Time, plus the faithful practice of the *17 Daily Exercises*, will make a difference, but even now, when those inexperienced fingers are wavering into action, strive for a smooth expressive technique as you move from one note to the next. This involves several things. A beginner can't hope to master them in a morning but even a beginner should bear them in mind.

First, an expressive technique involves a certain regard

for the flute. Touch your instrument gently, with a caress rather than a hammering. Don't bash the keys or release them with a thump, because such rough and ready vigour only kills off the life in the sound. There must be life in the sound for the whole period of its existence.

Second, work for an even touch on the keys – not a confident handling by strong fingers in easy positions while weak fingers in difficult positions creep to find the key and linger there uncertainly, but a controlled evenness from one note to the other.

Third, not only must each note sail forth with the same strength and assurance as its neighbours, but the transitions between notes must be smooth – no pauses, no silences, and no jerkiness to interrupt the flow. One way to help ensure this is to see that your fingers don't flap around too extravagantly. Agility is one thing, wasted energy another. Practise hand positions which keep the fingers near the keys and ready to operate with the minimum of fuss.

All three factors contributing to smooth finger technique can be summed up in one word: control. We are back to the Victorian parent. The first, second, third and last way to control your muscles (or breathing, or pitch) is practice. I have a thing or two to say about practice later on, and some exercises to recommend, invented by clever gentlemen who have given thought to flute-playing. In the meantime, listen hard to what you are doing, find your faults, do your best to correct them.

It could be that you need help in the enterprise, and for this you must turn to your teacher. At this point in your career, I can wish you no better luck than a skilful, amiable, patient teacher who knows the difference between nice sounds and unsatisfactory ones; who can tell you which notes you play well and which need work; and, above all, who can inspire you with enthusiasm for the flute and for the beauty of the simple sounds that even a beginner can get out of it. Such a teacher is an inspiration for life. I was lucky to find three in my formative years: Muriel Dawn, John Francis and Geoffrey Gilbert.

Nine
Tone

As well as being a pleasing sound, music has to say something. It has to express some emotion, light-hearted or wistful, satirical or pleading, serene or agitated – there is a whole Roget's Thesaurus of nuances to be got out of the notes a flute can produce. And the only way to make sure these nuances come out of the notes is to put them there in the first place.

Expressiveness

In this matter you have two responsibilities. One is to play so that the sound reflects your individual qualities. The expressive player, in my view, is simply one who knows where he is at and is in touch with his feelings. Naturally this ego-trip has to be subordinated to the character of the music. I don't want your feelings, however fine, riding roughshod over the composer's intentions. What I *do* want is your personal appreciation of those intentions to be heard in the way you play. Expressiveness can come only from within yourself, and if you shrink from playing the flute with the involvement of your own individuality, you will never develop expressiveness at all.

I have listened to many flute players who have been well trained, technically speaking, but have not learnt to project their personalities – or even, perhaps, to understand their personalities. Getting to know yourself is an important part of playing an instrument, for how can you communicate with an audience if you are not sure yourself what your music is saying? Often when I have asked students what they were thinking of when they played a sound that to me seemed unsuitable, the answer has been 'I wasn't thinking of anything.' That way lies dreariness and confusion. Don't watch the world pass by as you play, but think hard, think often, and if possible think to the purpose.

How exactly you set about getting to know yourself, I leave to you. Each person has a method of finding self-awareness, whether it is a body technique such as the Alexander Technique or yoga, or a more sedentary and cerebral approach like meditating or reading, or even simply by contact, abrasive or otherwise, with the rest of the human race.

As far as the narrower ambition of playing the flute is concerned, I am in no doubt about what you should do. It is a point I have made before and may yet do so again in the future, but I don't apologize for this repetition; it is important enough to merit being hammered home. If you are to have a certain sound at your fingers' and lips' end, it has to be in your head in the first place. Therefore an early task is to stretch your knowledge of what a flute can do. Don't be content to imitate the fellow two doors down who plays the flute in his spare time, but buy a record by a really top player and, in listening carefully to it, fire your imagination and ambition.

Sharpening your response to music (and thereby improving your own expressiveness) involves much listening to good performance, by other instrumentalists and singers as well as flute players. It is instructive to compare several interpretations of the same piece, and so widen your ideas of what is possible. I would like to insist on this a little, because in my teaching experience some clever young players stop short of real expressiveness and merely reproduce (in a very well-educated manner) the notation and dynamics on the printed page. Whether they do this because it's the lazy way out, or because in their humility they don't like to trespass on the private property of a Bach or a Debussy, the result is a literalness that does not endear the music to the listener. But spare a moment's pity for the poor composer: he has to have some way to write down his music for others to play, and convention restricts him to a bunch of notes on a stave. Shakespeare was limited to the letters of the alphabet, in various conventional arrangements, but just think what meanings and feelings an accomplished actor can bring out of those symbols. *You* are the actor now. It is your job to find the intention behind the marks on the page, so that you make a musical, not simply a mechanical, statement.

Your other responsibility is, of course, to learn the techniques which allow you to put across the emotions in your heart and soul. First among these techniques is control of tone.

At this point, a definition or two seems in order. The language of speech is too blunt an instrument to analyse music, which is why demonstration and example, especially by the best performers, are so important in this game. But at the moment the blunt instrument is all we have, and we must make the best of it. In blunt fashion, then, 'sound' is simply the basic noise, good or bad, that you contrive to produce. Your aim is to make it beautiful or at any rate as painless as possible. 'Tone' is the sound deliberately produced, which by hard work becomes flexible enough to express many different things. The next subtlety, 'colour', changes the metaphor from hearing to seeing, and therefore some people prefer to use the word 'nuance', which has the advantage of vagueness. But I shall stick with 'colour', by which I mean the innumerable different effects you can produce out of your well-trained tone.

Let's now give some thought to how the sound can become tone, and tone bring forth a multitude of different colours.

Flexibility of tone

Tone on the flute is, in my view, directly related to singing, and, in this exploration of the subject, I suggest you profit from the singers' example. When warming up, a singer will use vowel sounds only, rather than words. Each of these vowels has, as well as a distinct sound, a different colour, which the flute player can reproduce although he does not make the actual sound. Bright colours are made by the more closed-up vowels said at the front of the mouth, dark colours by the open vowels said at the back. Say a series of words to yourself, moving from closed-up to open, thus: flit, fleet, fled, flat, flute, float, flask (with a long 'a', London's pronunciation, not Manchester's). Note the different feel of these vowels inside your mouth. From now on you can forget the words and just use the vowel sounds.

Without your flute, sing a major scale using the sound 'u' as in 'flute'. Once you have done this exercise a few times, you will be well familiar with the mouth's internal arrangements for producing the sound 'u'.

Now try the same scale on the flute, but keeping the inside of your mouth in the u-forming position. This involves a degree of contortion, for the lips are no longer rounded but stretched. However, it can be done. It is important to keep the embouchure firm in order to compensate for the looseness and open feeling inside the mouth. Some flute players have got half-way to using vowel sounds to help them, but don't make the most of the trick because the flute is not held firmly and the connection point (the lip on the lip-plate) is too loose. The flute should never bounce up and down at this point of connection. This causes unfocused tone, rather breathy and not pleasant to listen to, and not centred enough to be able to create colours with.

Now another exercise. Take two vowel sounds, this time 'u' as in flute and 'a' as in flask. Alternate these two sounds, first singing, then when you have reminded yourself of the effect of each on your mouth and throat, with the flute. The big problem is the attack. At first, the alternating sounds are not easy to produce, so for starters try just the attack. Keep at this exercise until it sounds exactly the way you want it from the first micro-second of its existence. What we are after is a beautiful beginning, in addition to a beautiful middle and a beautiful end.

In this way, working through the range of vowel sounds, paying attention to the full length of the note, you will learn to control the tone. The aim is a pleasant, singing, happy sound which, to begin with, is sustained on a single note. That done, it is time for an exercise for controlling a line, and here two new factors come in to complicate matters: the fingers, which should be gentle, and the lips, which should be flexible.

Flexibility of the lips

Some people say the lips should not move at all when one is playing. All adjustments, they teach, should be made by the diaphragm. This seems to me a very cumbersome way to go about things, and about as sensible as trying to pick something up off the floor without bending. The contraction of the diaphragm tends to produce a bump in the sound which makes it difficult to phrase smoothly. The lips are a more subtle instrument altogether.

Angle of air-stream (Flute shown in cross-section at blow-hole)

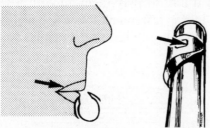

Arrows show air-stream aimed at tone-producing edge of blow-hole
Angle air-stream up a bit for high notes

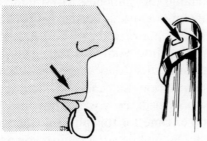

Blow down into the flute for low notes

99

According to my school of thought, it is not possible to play low B with the same embouchure as B two octaves above. You have to blow a fraction deeper into the flute for the low notes, you have to open out a fraction for the top ones.

But – by way of general warning and reminder – the movement of the mouth should not be visible. Flexibility in this context does not mean looseness. The embouchure remains tensed and the adjustments to it are so tiny as to be hardly perceptible even to yourself.

As you can imagine, it takes some doing to master these hair's-breadth adjustments, but since they are crucial in the production of a good tone, the sooner you make a start the better. What I recommend is daily exercises for lip flexibility, based on the principles laid down by Marcel Moyse in his book, *De la Sonorité*.

Begin by playing with the best tone you can muster – a middle note, for example B♮ in the second octave. Then move down to B♭, hoping for the same result; then down a further half-tone to A, comparing it for sound with the first two and trying to play them all with a similar tone; and carry on in this fashion all the way down the flute and up again, striving the while to get a similar sound on each note played:

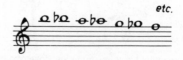

While listening for sameness of sound, discover for yourself what embouchure is needed for each note and the minute differences between them. Your aim must be so to absorb the feeling into your lips that, automatically and without conscious effort, they shape themselves to whichever note is in question. Since all the notes are going to be in question sooner or later, you have plenty of discoveries to make. It takes time for this physical control to become automatic, but meanwhile you can give yourself a test now and again. Stop anywhere in mid-exercise and check that embouchure. Also you should concentrate on notes that prove difficult. If you don't really know the shape of your embouchure for such a note, stop, find out, and memorize it for every future encounter with that note.

Now – still crawling up and down the registers in half-steps – practise making crescendos and diminuendos. Start as softly as you can on the chosen first note; make a crescendo; begin the next note at the volume just reached and make a diminuendo; and so on and so forth, thus:

The next thing to tackle is sustaining tone across larger intervals, beginning modestly with a third and going on to fourths, fifths, sixths, etc., always trying to produce the same quality of sound and without any unevenness on the way. There should be a clean break as each note begins and ends. There should be no extraneous noises between them, an unfortunate phenomenon which occurs when the fingering is uneven and the lips not properly adjusted to play succeeding notes. The ultimate aim is to be able to switch from the low notes to the high notes without any problem. This is difficult because it demands the greatest flexibility of the embouchure (although still unnoticeably slight to outsiders). You have to move your lips in mid-jump, so that they are in the right shape before you begin to play the distant note across the divide. It takes some doing, and re-doing, and re-re-doing after that to get your embouchure to this advanced stage of flexibility and control.

Long notes, first moving by semi-tones, then in scales, intervals and chord patterns, are the best way to achieve it. This is a general recommendation which you neglect at your peril. But there are also particular problems that need special attention.

One is the upper register, usually the least developed on the flute. It takes more air-pressure to blow with sustained and controlled strength at the top of the flute's range, and there are no short cuts to doing it well. You have to practise. At the other extreme, the low notes can be such a problem that maybe you are tempted to congratulate yourself for getting them out at all, never mind how. But something more is required. They have to have a meaning. While you try to make them sound nice, let me give you a word or two of warning and encouragement. Don't force the low notes. They have their own colour range, which has not got the strength of the range a couple of octaves higher. Be resigned to the fact that some loss of strength is involved in descending to the lowest notes, but still strive to give them all the flexibility and beauty of tone they are capable of expressing.

During the exercises outlined above – which I trust will be part of your daily routine from this moment on – three or four things will be improving simultaneously. The most intangible is the training of your ear. It is becoming familiar with the basic patterns of the intervals. Secondly, your fingers are learning their places on the flute and improving their agility. Thirdly, and indeed the main point of all this effort, the embouchure is acquiring flexibility in adjusting to the different notes. And lastly, as a consequence of all that has gone before, the tone quality is improving – or so I hope.

Playing *pp* and *ff*

The trouble with manuals of instruction is that they take things one at a time, like a man going steadily upstairs to reach his destination. But flute-playing is not a man going upstairs. It is an army advancing on all fronts in a well planned military campaign. In this straightforward attempt to plot the campaign, we have been obliged to defer consideration of some matters of vital importance. One of them is volume.

So now, if you will bear with me, I want you to go back to the single note. It has much to teach you yet, and the next lesson is to practise it at different volume levels.

Choose a note and play it to a count of, say, five with a normal dynamic. Stop, then play it again, reducing the volume slightly while keeping the sound alive. Again stop, and again reduce the volume. At each repetition the note should be almost, but not quite, as loud. There is no point in playing at a certain dynamic and then diminishing it by half. For real expressiveness, you need mastery of all the minute gradations of volume, from the just audible to the really startling. So, when you have got the note as soft as you can without loss of vibrancy, reverse the direction of the sequence, playing a fraction louder at each repetition until you reach your limit. As you practise the limits will get further apart and the intermediary levels more numerous and closer together.

You will notice that flexibility of the embouchure is important in this exercise too. A faster air-stream through a smaller hole is needed for loud playing, a slower stream through a larger opening for soft.

I suggest you choose one note for this exercise – but it should not always be the same note. Bit by bit all the notes that exist should be covered. A lot of people think it's a great thing to be able to play loud on the low notes. It's also a great thing to be able to play soft on the low notes. The same goes for the high ones. Therefore this technique of soft to loud should be practised in the three registers.

Going to extremes is very important. When you reach the soft end of the sequence, play *very* softly; at the loud end blow for all you are worth. Neither is easy for beginners, particularly as a beautiful sound has to be preserved throughout; but of the two, soft playing is the more difficult. Anyone with breath enough can make some sort of an impact by playing loudly, but to play with clarity, musicality *and* softness takes a great deal of control and a great deal of strength from inside. For this reason, these beginner's exercises can be of great service to you, so long as you practise them faithfully and seriously. As I have suggested before, in improving technique it helps enormously to have the sound you want to produce already in your head: it is as if the *imagining* of a sound somehow teaches the anatomy to get that sound out. In my imagination, a soft tone is white and a loud or hard tone is highly coloured, with an edge to it supplied by giving the vowel sound a nasal touch. These things are hard to explain. Your best plan is to listen and to copy. But choose a good model to copy from.

It is not a bad idea to spend some minutes every day on these abstract exercises for volume levels. However, since man does not live by single notes alone, I recommend that you cheer yourself up from time to time by making tunes serve the purpose. There are certain tunes which can only be played loud, and certain others which can only be played soft. And then there is a third category of tune, for example Handel's *Largo*, which survives being played at either end of the dynamic sequence. Playing the *Largo* at a dozen different volume levels should keep you busy for a day or two.

Velocity

Now we turn our attention to the fingers. Having spent so much time holding down a single note, they may have rusted into position and need limbering up. Again the progress is gradual, this time from slow to speedier. Take a simple exercise like this:

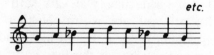

The point of this exercise is evenness. Whatever tempo it is played at, each note should be the same length and have the same tone as the one before and the one after. Take it slowly to begin with, then speed it up. (The point is to play these exercises several times.) And be careful always to use a light finger touch, gently guiding your fingers from one note to the next. It is very important not to disturb the sound by heavy uneven fingering.

When you can play this exercise smoothly, try another one:

As you can see, such exercises are the flute's equivalent of five-finger routines on the piano, a basic training to make your fingers do what you want at speed.

Vibrato

Vibrato is another subject on which experts violently disagree, and all of them are right. If one thing rather than another expresses the individual, it is vibrato. By way of demonstration, get a couple of records of Jascha Heifetz on violin and Maria Callas singing. Heifetz has a very intense vibrato, Callas a wide and slow one, and clearly, though they have nothing in common, both are using vibrato properly. There is no last word on what vibrato should be used, or how it should be varied to suit the music. These decisions are made by a player's own musicality and individuality. But I am certain enough about one or two things to chance being dogmatic here.

For a start, I am in favour of vibrato in general. There is a high-minded school of thought which holds that flute music should have the same purity of sound as an English boy soprano. Therefore it must not vibrate. Vibrato (these people say) makes the sound too sexy, too sensuous, and thus lowers the tone generally. I do not agree. In my view, vibrato gives life to the sound, allows for intensity, and helps a player to focus. Occasionally the music calls for stillness, and then a note or two or a phrase can be played without vibrato to advantage. But as a rule music without vibrato is a pretty lifeless thing.

A second belief of mine is that if the vibrato never varies, neither does the life of the music, and the result is rather tiresome and tedious. Some people think vibrato should have a regular speed. Others clearly demonstrate that it should not. The human body has a range of intensity of life, from sleeping peacefully to running the hundred yards' sprint. Music needs this too. But the intensity should always be intended and under control. The ultimate target is to master a whole variety of speeds of vibrato, on every note and at every volume level.

Thirdly I hold that work towards this target should begin early. Vibrato should be taught as soon as possible, partly because it sounds nice and so encourages beginners, partly because it helps them get the sound more in focus.

What is vibrato and where does it come from? Vibrato is the pulse of the sound brought about by the rapid alteration of more or less forceful pressure of the breath. Where it comes from – that is to say, what part of the breathing equipment actually operates this alternating pressure – I often wonder myself. The received wisdom has it that the muscles of the diaphragm are responsible, but I think this is not true at all or at least not the whole truth. Try it for yourself. Play your favourite note, making ha-ha-ha pressures with your breath, slowly and separately. Where in your body do you feel most distinctly the sensation of pressure? If you are a well-taught, obedient, respectful kind of youngster, you will say you feel it in the diaphragm. But I take leave to doubt the evidence of your senses. My own senses tell me that the muscles of the throat are responsible for controlling the pressure, and the diaphragm is merely quivering in sympathy. Moreover I think that players who cultivate a forward vibrato get excellent results from it.

So let's begin with the ha-ha-ha – a sound made in every language of the world, so you should have no problems with it. Blow a single note, making ha-ha-ha distinctly and separately. Blow it again with a faster ha-ha-ha. Then again, still faster. And so, by degrees of acceleration, until it is really fast when you drop the 'h' and let the notes run together in a perfectly regular undulation of pressure. When you have done it as fast as you can, put the metronome up a notch and do it faster. What you are aiming to produce is a smooth shimmer on the top of the note. Here is the sequence you should follow.

At this stage of the game, perfect regularity is important. A wavering, uncertain, uneven vibrato is a bad habit which you may not acquire. Later, when you know more about flute-playing, a certain latitude may be allowed you in speeding up or slowing the vibrato on a note to express your interpretation. Meantime, work to control your vibrato; do not let it come out anyhow. To this day I go through these stages of vibrato from the separate ha-ha-ha to the ultra-fast run-together version, for about three minutes in morning practice. If you want to get it right, this is what you have to do. If you want to be able to play with a vibrato which can be fast, slow, or left out altogether, this is the method you have to use.

For beginners it has to be a mechanical exercise. They play the note and they supply a helping of vibrato, consciously, deliberately, and as it were automatically. This is unavoidable except for the rare few whose built-in feeling for the music takes control of their technique early on. But others should not be downcast. As skill improves, as experience of music widens, vibrato painlessly becomes a part of your performing equipment.

Problems remain, of course: how to sustain vibrato across a phrase, how to achieve an apparent vibrato on top notes and when playing fast at any register, how to adjust vibrato to slow music. There is no sure-fire way of beating such problems except practising vibrato until it is firmly part of your technique. One last word on slow music: the temptation here is to take time about things, playing with a languid, reflective vibrato in supposed sympathy with the languor and reflectiveness of the music. This is a mistake. The slow vibrato only slows down the pace more than you had intended. Vibrato gives an impetus to slow music, and for this reason it must be at a certain speed (although which certain speed I leave to your discrimination). Similarly, soft music needs a quicker vibration, for the softer the note, the more tension you need to keep it up.

Ten
Practising

'How much should I practise?' There's a question that has echoed pretty regularly down the years. The quick answer is 'More,' but one mustn't be flippant about a serious subject like practice. When a student asks me how he should practise, or for how long, I know he hasn't got to the stage of hearing himself objectively. Once you *have* reached that stage, you are in no doubt about what needs sorting out. What to practise, how to practise and for how long to practise follow from this judgment of your playing. But do not be ashamed or discouraged if you are not yet at that stage. Objective assessment can very largely be acquired – with practice. In fact, this is what practice is about: not just learning to manage an instrument skilfully and to read music, but 'learning how to learn', that is, being your own teacher to some extent, giving yourself so many marks out of ten and sternly demanding better things in the future. Practice directs you down two parallel tracks. One leads to the improvement of your performance, the other constantly raises your imagination (and therefore your judgment) of what a sound should be, and so constantly raises your expectations of yourself.

Although a lot depends on yourself, in practice as in other aspects of musicianship, there are some general rules for living. Surprising though it may seem, the first is that the beginner should not practise too much. Until you have begun to develop the basics of flute-playing, it is a mistake to practise on regardless, incorporating faults and weaknesses into your technique. There is a logical problem here, I admit. Only practice is going to correct the faults and weaknesses. The solution is to tackle things one at a time, to be patient, to be happy about small advances. How much practice a beginner should do is a little difficult to decide for a readership of all shapes, sizes and ages, but I suggest that for most of you somewhere between fifteen minutes and half an hour a day is enough. At this point in your apprenticeship, a lot depends on your teacher, who must assess the strength of your embouchure and other progress, and gradually lengthen practice-time accordingly. Once you have the basics under elementary control – holding the flute steady, finding the notes readily, with the breathing and embouchure organized – you will be able to concentrate on what you are playing, and then is the moment to begin practising for as long as you can stand it and the other demands of your life allow.

The schoolchild, who must study other arts, skills and branches of learning, and the amateur player with a living to earn between nine and five have a similar problem (or simplification) about practice: they must fit it in where they can. Matters are different for the full-time student who hopes to become a flute-player, perhaps even a musician in time. Here, I would like to address a few words to you. For you, practice is a large part of your job, your duty in life. Okay, you have other things to attend to – theory, harmony, solfège, etc., and, if you happen to be studying in Germany, even pedagogy (perhaps no bad thing if it teaches future performers that they are not the end of the world but shortly to be succeeded by the next generation). All these things are admirable and essential and so forth, but they are also obligations which your prudent professors don't allow you to escape. But practice is the element in the schedule which you decide for yourself, and how much of it you contrive to do during the working day illustrates not only your stamina but the scope of your ambition.

If you are satisfied with getting by or are waiting for the hand of God to rescue you from slipshod preparation, so be it, read no further. But if you want to reach the heights

– what I call the 'special communicative standard' – then practice must become part of your daily existence. It has to become so much a part of your life that it is practically indistinguishable from an instinct, an appetite, or even a compulsion. You must learn to *need* to practise, just as (without troubling to learn it) you need to eat and sleep. When practice has sunk into your routine to this extent, we are really getting somewhere.

You may think I am exaggerating, or demanding too much, or using stronger language than the occasion warrants. In fact, I am speaking from experience. Only too often (I won't say always, in case somebody sues me for slander) a performer graduates from college, gets a job, and stops practising. On the one hand he thinks he knows it all, on the other there isn't time any more. All the time he has is spent in a motorcar driving from one place to the next fitting in a quick concerto here and a symphonic poem there, and no room for reflection anywhere. Too many professionals practise conscientiously for four years of higher education and that's it. I know this is disillusioning for all you youngsters, but there is as bad to come. Even college students, who have aspirations but as yet no job, neglect their practice. Scrupulously they do their four or five hours a day in term-time, but come the holidays they leave their flutes and their music in the cupboard and take a break. Term begins again, back they go to school, and have to start all over again, because the muscles have taken a break too and got lazy. I urge you not to adopt this stop-and-start pattern. Youth is the time when the muscles are most easily trained, and therefore you must spend time *now* on training them, with no breaks to let them relapse into sloth and forget their skills. If you are a real musician, there is no such thing as a holiday. I practise the flute every day of my life, at home, on tour, in transit if necessary. But I want to be really good at it. If you want to be really good at it, you will do likewise.

What should practice consist of? I suggest that you begin each day with exercises for breathing, sonority, vibrato and tonguing (you'll read about tonguing in the next chapter), then do scales and arpeggios, next studies, and finally pieces. Probably three-quarters of the time should be given to exercises, scales, arpeggios and studies, and only the remainder to pieces. This is a general rule, of course, not an unalterable law. If you have a concert to prepare, the priorities will naturally be different. In a moment, I shall say a word or two about scales and arpeggios, but before we reach the detail, here are a few general suggestions.

First, be active in your practice. It's blow, blow, blow (and listen, listen, listen). It is not an exercise in meditation. Second, try to sound happy. Very few composers actually intend their music to be dreary. Most music is happy, and even sad music must have life in it. So get a bit of *joie de vivre* into the exercises to prepare yourself in advance with the expressions you are going to need. Recall the slogan, practice is for performance. Third, insist on a beautiful sound. As already indicated, your conviction should be that an exercise, a scale, or even a single note is *music*. Otherwise what is the point of playing them? To inflict boring sounds on the world? From the first note you play when you get up in the morning, try to fill the room with a happy, lively, beautiful sound. Lastly, don't leave any note unattended. The more attention you pay to every note, the better your whole performance is going to be.

Scales and arpeggios

The first thing I must insist on is the absolute necessity of using a method for practising scales and arpeggios, at least if you hope to become a professional player or a very accomplished one. I recommend Taffanel and Gaubert's method in *Méthode Complète de la Flûte*. Do not play scales out of your head, for this leads to sloppiness and self-indulgence. These two gentlemen spent a lot of time thinking about the difficulties of flute-playing and how to solve those difficulties. Take advantage of their hard work.

Choose your method and over the weeks and years memorize it.

Over the weeks and years you must learn all the scales. They are the grammar of the musical language. A great deal of music – particularly baroque, but up to and including our own day – is based on scales and arpeggios. If you learn to play them perfectly, you are half-way to mastering a piece before you even start it. At the Conservatoire in Paris students have to play through all the major and minor scales without stopping, once a week. It is a good idea. Even if you don't have a professor to make you do it, do it anyway. There should ultimately come a point in your life when you can play all the scales – straight, in different intervals, with different articulation – and when it should be almost impossible to make a mistake.

Is your spirit quailing before these counsels of perfection? Take it easy. The days of your life stretch ahead, and each one of them can bring you closer to target. But start now.

I suggest that beginners should practice scales in two octaves, for instance the scale of F major:

At this point, when you are really exploring the scale, you must of course play slowly. Speed comes later. Begin slowly, until the fingers and embouchure know their way up and down these two octaves. Keep to this speed for a number of days, then put your metronome up a notch and similarly practise at the new speed until it feels easy. Then put the metronome up a further notch. So, notch by notch and month by month, you will advance towards virtuosity in two octaves of F Major.

The next task is to extend F major up and down the whole length of the flute: up as far as it will go and down again all the way to middle C. Like a piano player, you begin with one or two octaves, but in time

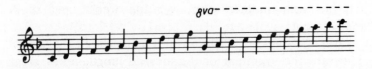

learn to cover the whole 'keyboard'. Don't think of the flute as having keys, think of it as a keyboard, and become familiar with every note upon it. When familiarity has been achieved, speed up the operation as outlined for the first two octaves. Some people advise slow practice of scales. I think this is crazy. It is like requiring a child of fourteen to speak the language of a child of four. I also think it is crazy to practise scales too fast. There is a simple way of deciding what speed you are capable of: if you go wrong consistently in a scale, then you are playing it too quickly. Slow it down to a tempo at which you get everything right, establish this, then increase the tempo.

So far we have not got beyond F major. But I am counting on sensible readers who will apply these words of wisdom to all the other scales as well. Some are easier than others, and it makes sense to tackle them first. A difficult scale such as E♭ minor, involving complicated fingering, you will have to play slowly for some time to come. There is nothing wrong with that. But don't base your entire programme of advancement on the speed of the slowest scale. If you wait till E♭ minor is up to standard before speeding up F major, you could hold your whole career back. Be reasonable about the tempo. Play the easy scales faster and the hard ones more slowly – and none of them faster then you can play them with profit. When E♭ minor does come out like a streak of lightning, it is very impressive – at least to fellow flute players who know the problems.

The next thing is to practise scales with different articulations. The next chapter is about articulation, so I shan't say anything about it here, except to remind you that practice is about making music and that you should articulate the scales with patterns of tonguing and slurring that actually occur in music.

A further complication: the scales should be practised in various intervals – thirds, fourths, fifths, and so on:

I shall have something to say later on about the need to train your ear to appreciate the different intervals. Meanwhile take my word for it that this apparent drudgery on the scales is in fact a short cut, if a laborious one, to musical mastery.

Then – and not before time, you may think – comes expression. You can play a scale soft or loud, happy or sad, with lots of sentiment or with virtuoso fireworks. Even if you have mastered only a couple of octaves of F major, you can begin playing them with different expressions. When you come to play bits of these scales in a piece, you will need to put feeling into them. Learn to put it in now.

Equally, arpeggios should not always be practised with the one boring expression, for they, like scales, are the basic structure on which music is built. They will likewise turn up in one form or another over and over again in the music you learn. And they, too, must be practised with this ultimate destination in mind.

Arpeggios can be a problem because they involve complicated finger changes which risk upsetting your hold on the flute – for example, the C major arpeggio, starting on low C and going up to top G. On the first note, all the fingers are in action so that it is easy to have a firm hold. For the next note, you have to move your little finger from the C to the E♭ key while lifting up the E key, and all this has to be done in one smooth operation, so that you don't disturb the embouchure. A lot of people have difficulty playing arpeggios because they make such a racket with their fingers that they miss the note with their lips. Therefore make a special point of keeping the flute absolutely still while you play arpeggios.

Focusing

Some players have the mistaken idea that scales and arpeggios begin and end with the fingers. They don't. Like any manner of speech, they begin and end with the expression behind them.

Control of expression involves concentration on the embouchure. When listening to young players doing sonority exercises, I have often noticed that they get a beautiful sound when the tempo is slow, but when it is quick the beautiful sound occurs only on the first note and the last note, and what comes in between is slightly out of focus. This comes from lack of attention to the embouchure.

When you play scales, you have to be sure that if somebody stops you right in the middle, that note will be just about the most beautiful thing ever heard. All the notes must be precisely in focus and related to each other. They get that way by practice – not too slow, not too quick, but at the speed where they all sound good.

A few late thoughts on practising

The next item on your daily schedule is studies, and this is important enough to have a section to itself.

However, before we abandon the subject of practice, I want to give you a few guidelines. First of all, I want to remind you to practise being happy while practising, even if you are in the worst mood in the world. The day may come when you must give a concert after flying the Atlantic or some equally tiring experience. Though your body groans, your spirit must feel good. Hence the need for happy practice from the start. Whatever you are engaged on – scales, exercises, studies – should really sound terrific.

Secondly, have fun. Since flute playing is hard work, practice too must be hard work, but it doesn't have to be grim. Everybody knows what all work and no play does to the character, even to the character of musicians for whom playing and working are closely related activities. So, when you have worked conscientiously on the exercises, take time to sight-read or to play something that you know and love. Enjoy the experience. Admire the lovely sounds you make. Such moments feed the inspiration, make the hard work worth-while – and encourage you to get back to the grind next day.

The third guideline follows from this, in a way. Practice has to be a regular, and if possible a daily, activity, but it is not penal service. If one day you find it absolutely impossible to concentrate, don't waste time by filling in the appointed hour (or whatever) with fruitless effort, but take a rest, or a walk, or a cup of coffee, until you are in a fit state to be properly absorbed in what you are doing. On the other hand, if inspiration and flowing creativity suddenly overtake you, don't feel you have to stop just because the usual time is up, but carry on, for the rest of the day, if you have the stamina.

We are all human beings. When people make this sort of observation, they are generally trying to excuse shortcomings. But I suggest that the remark can serve the other side of the argument. Precisely because we are human beings, we can conquer shortcomings by summoning up willpower, self-discipline, and – as a last resort – ingenuity. Like the rest of you, I know the feeling of getting up in the morning disciplined to do anything. I understand very well that practice is sometimes an unseductive thing to have to do. As I say, there are times when persistence is useless, but I hope such times are rare. For other reluctant moments, I offer this ingenious suggestion: think to yourself, okay, there's no way I'm going to be able to practise today, so instead I'm going to *play*. I shall treat these exercises and studies as if they were just the greatest music ever written (which very often they are definitely not) and I shall play them as if there were an audience out there which had paid for the privilege of hearing me.

Little tricks like that do wonders for the morale and, what is more, for the music.

Don't, however, become so obsessed with practice that you stop developing as a person, and only develop as a practitioner of a D major scale in thirds. If this happens, you won't be worth listening to, never mind knowing. You can no more live on practice than on sleeping or eating twenty-four hours a day. So make time for other people's music, other arts, friends, sports, pastimes – all the enjoyments of a mature and rounded human being. Cultivate your experience of life outside music and the flute. How you play reflects who you are, so the richer your personality, the more interesting your playing is liable to be. I include this stricture against too narrow a concentration on practice out of a scruple for completeness, and to correct the impression on delicate sensibilities of the stern warnings given earlier. But in my experience, it is a stricture most people can afford to forget. Too much practising is not a widely committed fault.

The remaining guidelines are of a more practical and less philosophical nature.

– Don't always play things at full speed. Of course you must learn to play fast, but from time to time slow the tempo down so that you can really hear what is going on.

– Don't play past the difficulties that crop up. Play the difficult passages over and over – not ten times, but a hundred times, if that is what it takes.

– Pay constant attention to detail.

– Don't be afraid to test out different routines.

– Get it firmly into your head, for now and evermore, that practice is, ultimately, your own responsibility. It is up to you to discover your problems and the solutions to your problems. Other people will hear the quality of (let us hope the improvement in) your playing, and may have helpful observations to offer, but it must be your aim, in practising, to become the first judge of your own cause.

All the above is addressed to serious students. By this I don't mean just full-time students who hope one day to make a living by the flute, but also the weekend and leisure-hour players who play the flute for the good and sufficient reason that it adds to the enjoyment of life. Clearly, amateurs with other demands on their time can't spend the long hours on the flute needed to reach the highest virtuoso standards. Don't let this depress or frustrate you. There is excellence, satisfaction and fulfilment to be won, provided you care enough, and at any level it is an achievement for the human race at large. Work out a mini-routine of practice along the lines suggested, and look forward to improving at your own pace.

Remember, amateur, that you are a useful and special person. I know you get a lot of fun out of the flute, but apart from this you are a valuable individual, especially to the profession of flute players. We value you for your enthusiasm and for your discrimination, which finds and encourages young talent and generally helps to give the flute a more highly regarded place in the world of music.

Eleven
Articulation

Articulation is a big heavy word for a very simple thing. In our context it refers to speech. How you articulate the English language means how you organize your tongue, vocal cords and so forth to say words. It also means the effect of those words. The articulate person has a way with words, he or she can express himself or herself, he or she is eloquent. The same goes for the flute. Articulation means the techniques for playing legato or staccato, and it also means the eloquence which these techniques allow.

So this chapter is really about learning to play with expression, a wide subject involving your heart, soul and personality. But we shall begin at the technical beginning.

Tonguing

Most musicians use the Italian word 'staccato', meaning separate. The French say 'détaché', equally meaning separate. And we British have an expression of our own, 'tonguing', because it is the tongue which brings about the desired effect. By briefly touching the hard part of the palate above the teeth, the tongue interrupts the air-stream, so *separating* the notes from one another. How 'separate' is separate remains to be decided, or rather to be discovered and learnt, for tonguing covers a variety of speeds and a range of attack from hard to soft. What staccato does *not* mean is short. One direction for short is the string term pizzicato and this is sometimes used for special effect, but too often young players confuse the one with the other.

There are different devices for learning to tongue a note. Some teachers advise their pupils to say 'tu', others prefer 'du', others yet again 'tee'. The reason for these minor disagreements between experts is that half of them don't speak the same language to begin with, and even those who do come from different regions and speak with different dialects. My own preference is the French word 'tu', which has a rather special sound unknown on this side of the Channel. If you have never heard it said, and would like to try my system, you will have to check with a French teacher. The reason I prefer 'tu' to the alternative is that it brings the tongue well forward and shapes the lips into a position more natural for flute-playing. Every French person says 'tu' without pain or thought, which may explain why France has produced so many good flute-players over the last few centuries.

Anyway, having chosen one of the above options, try blowing a note while repeating 'tu-tu-tu' (or whatever) for the whole length of a breath. Do this as slowly as you like to begin with, keeping the repetition even in duration and intensity. From this point there are two separate paths of progress to follow. One is to speed up the tonguing. The other is to learn to vary it, from the least, softest and gentlest touch of tongue to palate to the real hard attack with zing in it. Explore the possibilities first, then master them bit by bit.

For very fast staccato or détaché playing, double-tonguing is needed. This involves the alternation of 'tu', made by the tip of the tongue against the hard palate, with 'ku', made by the middle of the tongue against the back of the roof of the mouth. It is less of a tongue-twister than it sounds at first. Again, blow the note of your choice, this time saying as you do so 'tu-ku-tu-ku-tu-ku' etc. until your breath gives out. Practise doing this until you get it really fast. When I was a beginner, I was taught to practise 'tu' and 'ku' separately, 'tu' on one note, 'ku' on another, until both were in a fair state of readiness when they were put together. I have come to believe that this is not a good idea, and that 'tu-ku' can be run in harness from the moment a learner attempts double-tonguing.

Having learnt to tongue and to double-tongue, put the technique to use in your practice of scales or of exercises for finger velocity. Experiment with different sorts of staccato – playing now a brisk one, now a very lively one, now something smoother altogether – in preparation for the pieces this technique is designed to serve. Avoid going overboard on staccato. There is a certain point where it ceases to be a source of enjoyment and becomes a pain in the ear. In all circumstances it should sound nice, easy and generally happy.

Legato

A most important factor in a nice legato (apart from not letting your tongue get in the way) is the action of the fingers. If there is to be a stillness in the music, the keys must not be clapping up and down like the keys of a rackety typewriter. Everyone can play from one note to another – which is what legato is – but it is going to sound great only if the notes are caressed. The feeling of smoothness, of tenderness, of serenity, should be inside you, transmitting the caress through the fingers to the keys.

Indian flute players are particularly good at legato playing on their *bansari*. These bamboo flutes have seven holes in them, one for blowing, six for the notes, and no keys to intervene. They can glide from one note to the next, making slides not possible to us, producing the lingering legato that is their speciality.

In contrast, we have keys and must cope with them. So we make as little motion as possible with the fingers, and coax the music out of the flute.

One of the best ways to practise legato is to play pieces which demand this singing, 'bel canto' smoothness. Examples are Handel's *Largo*, or 'The Swan' from Saint-Saëns's *Carnival of Animals*, or Gounod's *Ave Maria*.

Articulation

Presuming you have now learned tonguing and slurring, the next task is to use these techniques in conjunction with each other. Articulation on the flute boils down to a certain combination of tongued and slurred notes, in the patterns common in standard classical pieces. To play the pieces, you have to know the patterns, first of all in the abstract.

Again, the scales can serve your turn. Give them different articulations from time to time, for example two notes tongued, two slurred, or three and three, or one and two.

That should keep you busy for a week or two, but believe me, it is time well spent in view of the Mozart Concerto looming on the horizon where these patterns of articulation will be required.

That said, I think one can be too pedantic about articulation. The French really go to town on it and work out all sorts of permutations to drive their students crazy. They invent patterns that no composer ever uses – unless in an examination piece for the Conservatoire. For example, the *Fantasie* for flute that Fauré wrote for the *Concours*: it has articulations in it that he never used anywhere else. I guess he just went along to the flute professor at the Conservatoire and asked what was difficult on the flute. So the professor listed a few problems – long notes, trills, détaché scales, other complicated articulations – and Fauré noted them down, thanked the professor, and went off and cooked a musical soup. Well, if you can get the better of the *Fantasie* you will be equal to most articulations, with a few never otherwise required of you.

Attack

Tonguing has two functions. In addition to staccato playing, it is the method by which attack is given to a note. For a nice, clean, clear opening to a note or phrase, launch it on a 'tu'. As with tonguing for staccato, there is a range of energy of attack to be learned. Not every piece of music starts with the boldness of Beethoven's *Emperor Concerto*. Not every opening 'tu' needs the same vehemence. I can only advise you to decide for yourself the strength of attack in any given circumstances, and to train the tongue to obey your instructions.

How to begin *L'Après-Midi*

There are people who say that every first note, at the beginning of a piece or, after a rest, at the beginning of a phrase, should be given attack by tonguing, vigorous or otherwise according to circumstances.

In my view the note should sometimes be played with the embouchure open and the tongue well out of the way. A comparison can be made with a singer who starts a note on a vowel rather than with a consonant. This has the advantage that the note can begin very softly and swell into more assertive existence as it proceeds.

The beginning of *L'Après-midi d'un faune* needs this sort of treatment. Here is one of the most famous flute solos, and one of the most difficult because the composer didn't make allowance for breathing. But a start on overcoming the difficulties can be made by getting the first note right. It is my practice, and therefore my preaching, to play it without tonguing. Get ready to play the note with the embouchure open and just blow gently until it floats out from nowhere.

Now, the problematic breathing. I have no technical tricks to suggest, but only general encouragement to do your best, make your best better, and above all don't be frightened of the task. Here is a tale, exemplary rather than cautionary I hope, from my own experience.

When I first played the *L'Après-midi* solo with the Berlin Philharmonic, which is generally considered an orchestra of grown-up players equal to the stuff they are meant to be doing, I was aghast at the markings in the first phrase of the solo in the music I was given. It had so many breathing spaces and emergency breaths and Red Cross parcels posted on to it that it looked more like a refuge for asthmatics than a challenge to flute players. So I thought to myself: I am no longer ten years old. I'm a grown man. The composer intended this phrase to be played in one breath and played in one breath it shall be. In the event I nearly, literally, blacked out; but having done it once, I did it more easily the second time. Like four-minute milers, you have to have a goal to beat. It set me thinking. I thought, why stop here? Why not do this with other music? And so I cut down on unnecessary breathing all round.

To bring off a breathing feat of this sort, you need to be prepared. Your mind has to be quietly confident, and your lungs filled to capacity, with an added final snatch of breath on top, as described in the earlier passage in breathing. Then without articulating just let the music emerge. Since it is a solo, you won't have any competition, except the audience holding conversations with itself, so with luck and a well-educated audience that first faint thrilling thread of sound should be heard.

A final word. The solo of *L'Après-midi* is played sitting down. So practise it sitting down, unless you have to play it in a dance band.

Playing slow movements

The truth in slow movements is harder to grasp, probably because it is more profound. Fast movements titillate the senses. The message comes over easily. Of course, fast movements confront the player with greater technical problems, but to compensate for its apparent lack of technical difficulty, the slow movement demands a super-eloquence, an extra expressiveness.

The same comparison can be made about speaking. There are some brilliantly articulate public speakers who really sock it to you, *allegro* or even *presto*, making a powerful overall impact but leaving you too dazzled to remember what they actually said. Others give the listeners time to digest. When Churchill told the British in the last war that they were up against it and he intended them to survive the experience, he spoke *largo* and *lento*, giving the nation time to reflect on his words. His message was profound, serious and needed absorbing.

So it is with slow movements. Their message needs to be heard and understood, which, from the player's point of view means first that he must understand it himself, and second that he must have the skill to put it over.

Don't think of slow movements as all belonging in the same grave, weighty category. Even J. S. Bach, composer of the sublimest slow music in the Western world, has given us relatively light-hearted slow music, and of course you have to bring a quite different habit of mind, thought and playing to later music, such as the *Entr'acte* in the third act of *Carmen* (which should be floating and singing), or the solo in *Daphnis and Chloë* (which is full of nuances).

You have to realize the expression, the feeling you are trying to create, and you have to get yourself in the mood to create it. This is sometimes a ticklish problem, because immediately after the slow bit you have to play, more often than not, something of a different mood entirely. The standard classical equipment was a quick movement, a slow movement, a minuet or whatever, and a fast movement for the finish. Your job is to be ready for all these changes of tempo, feeling and meaning, so you have to know beforehand what you want to say in each.

As for the articulation of a slow movement, ponder again the words on legato playing and especially remember to caress the keys rather than just putting them up and down. Articulation is about expression. If you play a slow movement with the wrong feeling, you are being inarticulate. If you have the right feeling but inexpert clumsy fingers and a tongue which does not know whether it is coming or going, whether a note is to be tongued or slurred, then, again, you are inarticulate. Understanding of music and the techniques to express that understanding must advance together, so that you do the composer justice and give your audience something worth listening to.

Twelve
Pitch

The first thing to establish is that you actually have a flute that is in tune. There are plenty around that are not in tune, but since Albert Cooper of London showed the way some other instrument makers here and there have begun to build flutes according to precise mathematical principles rather than by rules of thumb handed down the generations.

The basic mathematical fact concerns the relationship between the length of the tube and the sound it produces. Once this relationship is understood, a flute can be built at any pitch required. If you are considering buying a new flute, I would advise strongly against getting one at A440 (that is, 440 vibrations per second for A natural, in case this important detail had escaped your attention). The truth is that 440 is a pipe-dream of the English oboe player, which doesn't exist any more except in an English concert hall, and then only till the oboe player stops. I advise buying an A442, on the grounds that it is easier to adjust the pitch downwards if the flute is high than upwards if it is low. Pitch varies surprisingly across the world. The highest in my experience is in Germany, and it is considerably higher than the pitch in America. So adjustments sometimes have to be made at the frontier, but you need not trouble too much about changing pitch across countries until you become a wandering musician.

However, you too will surely have to alter the pitch from time to time. You may be lumbered with an out-of-tune instrument, which requires you to blow a little deeper into it on a note that is marginally high, or vice versa, to blow fractionally farther out of it on a note that is flat. Furthermore, it is not impossible that you will be accompanied by an eccentrically tuned piano with which you have to come to terms. And lastly you have to take account of your colleagues. They too can have problems with defectively tuned instruments.

Apart from the overall pitch of an instrument, other things in its making have to be taken into consideration, such as the placing of the holes (also based on mathematics) and how skilfully the whole thing is put together. If you want the best and can afford it, I recommend buying any flute made by Mr Cooper personally, or else a flute made by one of those companies using the Cooper scale, based on the proper mathematical calculations, which will then as a result be in tune. Mechanically at any rate you then have nothing to worry about.

Developing a sense of pitch

What you *do* have to worry about is your own appreciation of pitch. It is easier to sharpen this sense than many people imagine. Perfect pitch is a bit mysterious and magical and no doubt useful to have on occasions, but this fairy godmother's gift is not what we are after. What we are trying to develop is a feeling for the relationship between different notes. People say, 'Oh, I've no ear for music, I can't tell one note from another.' But get them to sing the first stave of *God Save The Queen* and nine-tenths of the population will do it perfectly. What they have absorbed without being aware of it is a first dim notion of the relationship between the notes, or as we musicians say, the intervals. That first dim notion can certainly become keener, with effort and experience, for all except the truly woodeneared. It is no more outside the ordinary person's capabilities than developing a sense of where the kerb is, or how far away one should be from the car in front, when learning to drive. Nobody has this sense until they learn to drive. Nearly everybody learns to drive, to some more or less adequate degree. Similarly, nearly everybody can improve their sense of pitch.

In working consciously for this improvement, there are three intervals which should be given special and persevering attention. They are: the octave; the fifth; and the fourth. All three are perfect intervals, by which I mean that there has been no well-tempered tampering with them to fit them into the octave. They are mathematically perfect, like a properly built flute. To get this perfect maths into your ear, you should practise a scale in octaves, or in fifths, or in fourths, slowly. Slow here means super-slow. You have to listen to what you are doing, you have to have time in which you can hear the next note in the sequence in your mind before you. play it. These scales should be repeated, with unflagging concentration and your ears at stretch, until the intervals have become a part of you.

Violin players have an unfair advantage in this business, because they tune in fifths, and so absorb the interval without really trying. You must really try. Once well launched on the fourths, fifths and octaves, add the other intervals to the practice schedule, perhaps testing them first against a piano – if you have a well-tuned piano at your disposal and a pianist on hand.

You will notice that the pitch of any given note alters according to how hard you blow. The harder you blow, the sharper it gets, a tendency particularly noticeable on high notes. To correct this tendency you must resort to the infinitesimal adjustments of the embouchure that have already been discussed a time or two in these pages. A minute drawing back of the jaw and an equally minute extension of the top lip will direct the air-stream deeper into the flute and remove the sharpness from the note. In this connection, remember that the pitch alters during the course of a crescendo or diminuendo. A flexible embouchure and an acute ear take care of the problem between them.

As I say, slow scales in the perfect intervals are the best

way to develop a sense of pitch. But there's no harm in being constantly aware of pitch, whatever musical pattern you happen to be playing. By now the scales and arpeggios should be ringing in your head, ready for immediate production. Your refined appreciation of pitch can be furthered by these exercises, at the same time as the lips acquire flexibility and the fingers grow more agile. May I remind you yet once more that a sound has first to be in your head if, subsequently, it is to come out of the flute.

Correct intonation is a very basic requirement for music, and therefore any effort made to achieve it is justified. However, the sort of intensive listening I suggest you practise brings added bonuses. In addition to a feeling for pitch, the ear learns to be discriminating about tone, colour and expressiveness. It learns the different colours of the different keys. For the keys have, as it were, personalities, as well as particular meanings for particular composers. For example, F major is by nature very bright, whereas D♭ is something else again. A minor is a comfortable key to play in, largely I think because of its traditional background. Bach and company in the eighteenth century wrote a lot of music for the flute in A minor, because it was easy to play on the old-system flute. So, by a technical accident, A minor has become a sort of home key for flute players. But there's no way you can stay at home for the rest of your life, so get acquainted with all the other keys too, and practise until every note in every key is okay.

Transposing

Transposing is terrific training for the hearing, not to mention the fingers. It is also a good way to develop a feeling for the instrument. Lastly, the ability to transpose is sometimes needed in an emergency – when the singer turns up on the night with voice strain and has to have everything put down a half-tone because he can't reach top C. Or like an experience of my own: I turned up at a recording session one day to find that, whereas the score was in C, the piccolo parts were in D♭. I had to transpose everything there and then. For flute players it is a relatively simple operation. Think of the pianist's problems. Because they are constantly accompanying somebody or another, pianists are for ever transposing the most complicated music up and down the keyboard and they soon learn how to do it if they want to stay in business.

Stern necessity apart, transposing is fun. Take a short, simple tune, a folk song for example, or a few bars from a Handel sonata, and play it in (say) G. Then shift the whole thing a semitone higher and play it in A♭. Don't stop there, but drop down to F#, and then gradually take this folk song or whatever through all the keys that exist. It is better not to write out the transpositions, if you can manage without a written reminder. It is not your ability to read music that is being tested by this challenge, but your hearing and your knowledge of the keys. In time you will be able to transpose quite fluently. When that point is reached, your sense of pitch (among other skills and talents) is really getting somewhere.

Thirteen
Studies

Studies have something in common with a dentist's drill. They find the weak place and drill away at it remorselessly. In the musical case, an aspect of technique is isolated – for example, a specific interval or a specific articulation – and presented to the player over and over again, modulating in and out of the keys, from beginning to end of the study. Such repetition builds stamina as well as obliging the player to pay thorough and sustained attention to whatever technique is currently under review. However, if you are going to profit from studies, comparisons with the dentist's surgery must be laid aside, so that you treat them as music. Some studies – what the French call *études* – are in fact pieces of music. Covertly concerned with some technical difficulty, they wrap up their purposes in a musical conception, with an introduction, a development, usually a recapitulation, and of course a basic melody moving through harmonic changes.

A more austere sort of study doesn't trouble to conceal its preoccupations with technique under melodic seductions. Examples are the studies based on scales and arpeggios and those for improving tones and colours. Nonetheless these too must be approached with the same musical seriousness that you bring to a well-loved composition. The good habit, which I hope you are learning, of never playing a single note, a scale or an arpeggio other than beautifully must be maintained in the practice of studies.

That's one generalization. A second is that studies offer a further chance to develop self-awareness, and particularly the ability to judge oneself objectively. This gift won't be granted to a passive student. It takes effort and commitment on your part to earn it. Naturally, teachers, other musicians and flute-playing friends can give aid and encouragement to clarify your mind and sharpen your hearing. Moreover, the studies themselves exist as objective tests of skill and musicianship, against which to measure your own abilities. This said, in the end it is how well you personally understand the studies and what you personally do with them that guarantee progress.

Progress may not be obvious overnight. Which does not necessarily prove that you are not trying, for people develop at different speeds and are born with varying quickness of comprehension. The end result matters more than how rapidly it is reached. Do not let your heart be troubled by the distance of the destination, or the obstacles strewn between you and it, but strive to make the most of studies and trust them to carry you in the right direction.

Don't be too modest in your demands on yourself. By this I mean that ambition is not likely to hold you back, but a humble resignation to mediocrity certainly will. If, as I hope, your critical faculties develop alongside your skill, you need have no fear that vanity will get out of hand. Equally, don't be afraid to ask the teacher for an assessment of your understanding of studies. The view of the more experienced outsider is always interesting and usually corrective. Besides, he may not have considered the matter in the detail you demand, in which case your question could be of not a little value to him as well as to yourself.

The opportunities for continual growth, even rebirth, given by music (and no doubt the other creative arts) never cease to amaze me. You too can experience that precious feeling of beginning again, of being renewed. Enjoy it and cultivate it, but don't take it as your disembarkation point. Always be open to reassessment and the possibility of further progress. If Einstein was half-way right, there is no end to the universe.

Beginners

The beginnings of the universe are not exactly established either, but your case is simpler. Having spoken so much about personal responsibility, I now have to set limits to it in your best interests. You should not work on technical problems out of your own head, unaided, any more than you did with scales and arpeggios. For beginners I recommend Marcel Moyse's book, *Le Débutant Flûtiste*.

To summarize the words of wisdom already spoken: take these studies seriously, respect them as ways to perfection, treat them as music.

At this point in your career you must rely for understanding on the guidance of your teacher. If he is patient and inventive, he will find ways to enlighten you. But already you can begin to do things for yourself. On our own behalf, therefore, always look for the purpose underlying a study, the aspect of technique it is designed to strengthen.

When tackling a new study, I believe you should begin by sight-reading it from start to finish, especially if it is written in an awkward key or if you see there are tricky finger changes ahead. This way you test your reading abilities and, what is more important, you find out your weaknesses.

Put to use what you have already learned about articulation, fingering, pitch and so forth, even if this does not yet amount to much. Supply the gaps with ingenuity and – if all else fails – imagination. By constantly puzzling out ways to solve problems, you become more committed to the study.

Try and figure out the harmonic patterns of the piece. Don't just observe key changes with the eye and the intellect but introduce to your ears the sounds they represent. Try to remember these sounds so that when your eyes next meet these keys or modulations, you will have a better chance of reading them at sight.

Practise the intervals for intonation, fluidity and overall clarity.

Repeat difficult finger passages over and over again to make sure your hearing and fingering are coordinated.

Memorize the study. If you put it through all the hoops listed above, you will soon know it by heart anyway. Just make sure you do. As the weeks pass, commit to memory the succeeding studies you tackle, so that in time you have a standard manual of flute-playing in your head, for instant reference on all occasions. Memorizing music is good for discipline, for ear-training, possibly for a future career as a teacher or a soloist. The teacher who knows the notes already inspires trust, the one who has to keep checking them does not. Soloists generally play without scores at concerts, so it is a good idea to get used to memorizing pieces as well as studies. But even if you never play in public, memorizing is an excellent education for the ear.

Lastly, when you have the study as familiar to you as your own name, have a bash at transposing it up or down a semitone.

Advanced students

The above is, as it were an outline scheme for making the most of studies. I have included it in the advice for beginners in the joint beliefs that practice should be serious from the start and that the simplest of studies can be richly exploited. The advice stands for advanced students doing advanced work.

My principal recommendation to you is to work on *De la Sonorité* by Marcel Moyse. To encourage you to do these exercises, my further comments will be based on them. For one thing, it is difficult to make useful observations across the whole range of technique, without an example here and there to link us with reality. For another *De la Sonorité* is an excellent piece of work. The odd thing is that this marvellous tool for aspiring flute-players came into existence rather casually. Moyse wanted money to go on holiday, so he put the book together, sold it outright for a certain sum of francs, and took himself off. But what he actually wrote, without knowing it, was something on the lines of *Zen and the Art of Flute Playing*. It takes about four years of playing these exercises every day before you begin to know what they are about and get the benefit of them. By that time you are no longer thinking about the technique of making a nice sound, because the sound is coming from within you. It automatically becomes you. And then you are in a position really to do something with the notes.

Before we get down to considering different aspects of technique, I should like to risk a generalization or two on tempo and volume. You may recall my insisting that you learn to play scales fast. For advanced students this is certainly a necessary skill. It is an exercise in getting your fingers working, not to mention your lips. Various studies to improve these aspects of technique can be found in Moyse's *Technical Studies and Exercises* and his *Daily Exercises*. These, once thoroughly learned, must be practised at speed.

But Moyse's sonority exercises must be played slowly, or super-slowly, so that you know exactly where each note on your instrument is – so that you don't just blow and move your fingers, but actually play each note as it passes. If you play too quickly, you don't have time to listen to what is happening and to regulate it and you do not educate your lips.

As for volume, the straight answer is: use your common sense. The character of the study is one factor to take into account. For example, one of the Moyse studies demands a repeated sequence of soft, medium loud, louder, really loud, then back through these gradations – demanding also the alteration of the vibrato along the way in the cause of musicality. Another factor is your own need to be expert at any volume, which implies practising to control each and every one of them to the thinnest shaving of a difference. However, if in practice you come across a real corker of a problem, don't play too softly so that you obscure it for yourself and for any chance listener, but get

the difficulty into the open loud and clear. Once you have
beaten it at full strength, you can afford to soften down
again. And remember, there is more value in playing
beautifully than in playing loud, or for that matter soft.
Never practise playing badly. You will only learn how to
do it, which is in nobody's interest, least of all those who
have to listen to you.

In no special order, here are examples of the sorts of
study you should be doing daily. Let's look first at some
exercises devised by Marcel Moyse. First, some for training
the embouchure to adjust to different notes and to go from
one note to another without interruption of the sound.

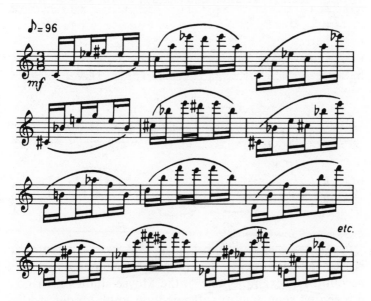

from *Technical Studies and Exercises* no. 3

When practising the following two exercises, discover how
your embouchure shapes for, say, B, B♭, B♭ an octave
lower, and all the other notes, and when you play, make
sure you fit the shape to the note very exactly. Otherwise
you don't get the best tone and your time spent doing
sonority is wasted. It requires thinking ahead, which you

from *De la Sonorité* no. 1

from *Comment j'ai pu maintenir ma forme* no. 7

have time to do, since these exercises are to be played slowly. For example, you are playing F and E♮ is coming up. Get the F established and think of the sound (and shape) for E. Having successfully made the transition once, practise it a few more times to get it really fixed in your head.

The above exercises for the embouchure also train the fingers while generally improving your command of tone. This is an admirable aspect of these studies: they take you thoroughly in hand and improve you in half a dozen ways at once. But for more specific fingering exercises try the sample opposite, from Moyse's *Scales and Arpeggios* – an essential book, the continuation of his equally essential *Daily Exercises*. As well as making the fingers stronger and more agile and precise, these studies are an opportunity for learning to get maximum effect with minimum movement.

From *Scales and Arpeggios*

Some of the exercises already mentioned have introduced technical problems that really stretch a flute player. The examples on pages 142–4 from *Daily Exercises* and *Tone Development through Interpretation*, exercise the embouchure, the fingers and the control of tone, while bringing in the further complication of extreme intervals. For me it is a big hassle to move from low to high or high to low, and it takes some years' practice to do it easily.

Broken Arpeggios, from *Daily Exercises*

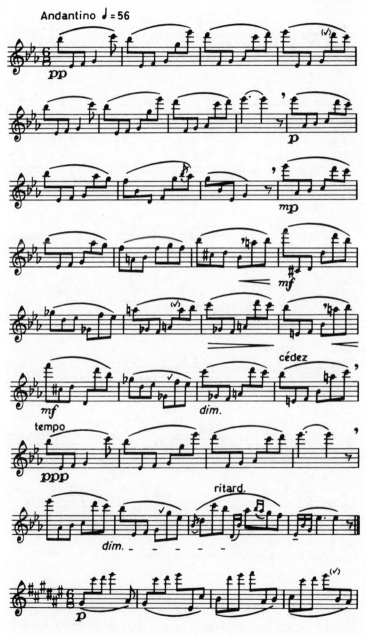

From *Tone Development through Interpretation*

Other specific problems are low notes (dealt with in the exercise on p. 145, from *Technical Studies and Exercises No. 1*), super-legato playing (see p. 146, from *25 Melodious*

etc.

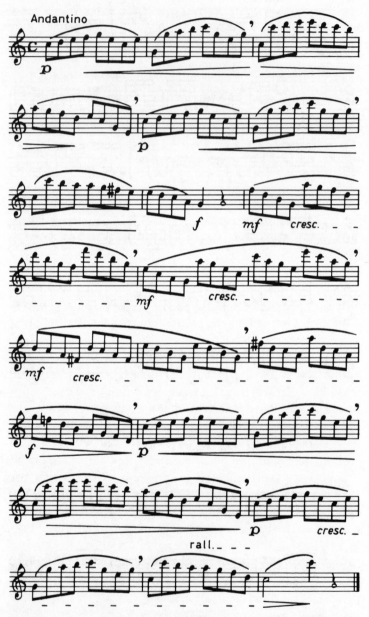

Studies No. 1) and trills (try this one, from Taffanel and Gaubert's *17 Daily Exercises* No. 17):

146

I have the impression that nobody practises trills properly. Studies which will deflate your complacency about trills are included in the book *Grand Liaison*.

But underlying all this improvement in technique, Moyse's studies are designed to help you make your playing more worth listening to. The way to this happy result is the hard road of control of lips, fingers and breathing to the point where they respond automatically to produce the sound (tone and colour) you intend. A really tough example occurs on page 23 of *De la Sonorité*, a page only the dedicated ever reach. In this study you take a single note and practise how many colours you can get out of it. As an advanced student you cannot be content with the first sound that comes out of the flute, just so long as it is in tune. For a start, it must be a healthy sound from the first micro-second of its existence, but secondly it must be a *chosen* sound. When you tackle a piece you have first of all to learn the notes, of course, but your next task is to think how you would like them to sound. There are many, many possible sounds, but unless you learn to make them now, you won't be able to choose

147

them in the future. Moreover you ought not to choose the colours at random, but rather in order to say something. Colour and expression are the same thing in this business. This particular study is a very good exercise in colouring. Using the same expression, you increase the volume by degrees, as if you were covering a wall with successive coats of paint. The wall still shows through the first coat, and even, though more faintly, through the second. With the third the colour is beginning to win, with the fourth it stands out, with the fifth it really hits you. So you put on a sixth and seventh just to make sure. It is this sort of nuance which Moyse's study perfects, so that you have it under control when you turn to Bach, Handel or Debussy.

Don't, however, neglect his other studies. You have to master all of them if you are to become a complete flute player.

And here I should like to stress something I have already spoken of: the character – almost I would say the meaning – of different keys. C major is to F major as green is to red. You must learn to feel the difference and to express it. A piece of music modulates through many keys, even if its title claims it is in A minor, for example. Its title is largely for identification purposes, so that you don't confuse it with some other composition. In fact, the music moves through many keys, and unless you appreciate these subtleties, you won't play it very well. Fortunately, *De la Sonorité* covers this aspect of flute-playing along with all the others.

How to put the benefit of practice into pieces

The basic rule is to relate practice to performance. Practice is not an end in itself. Generally it is done privately, furtively, and behind closed doors, but these circumstances must not blind (or deafen) one to the fact that practice is concerned with playing actual music to actual human beings. The lesson is that you should never sound as if you were *practising*, but always as if you were *playing*.

A way to ensure this is to keep an appropriate piece of music in mind when you are doing a given exercise. Say you are practising long notes. Think of a piece which includes such notes, for example Beethoven's *Leonora* overtures, and practise the exercise with that piece in view. In the middle of the long notes exercise, try a few notes of the piece. So the expression of your practice is carried into the piece, and the piece into the practice. Another example: say you are practising articulation of the 'two tongued, two slurred' variety. Think of a Mozart concerto which has a lot of this pattern in it, and play that scale or study to make it sound as like a Mozart concerto as you can.

Take this passage from the fourth daily exercise in Taffanel and Gaubert's *17 Daily Exercises*:

Compare it with these bars from the last movement of the *Flute and Harp Concerto* by Mozart. You could practically swap them over:

Playing, practising and developing technique

Bearing such similarities in mind helps to discourage the notion that studies are somehow a sub-species of music.

Developing 'touch'

To end this section, here are a couple of thoughts on the refinements of touch on the flute. The general rule remains that you should always touch the flute nicely. Respect your instrument. Never treat it with violence or aggression. But that said, different sorts of music demand a different touch.

This is perhaps more easily demonstrable in works for the piano. A fast movement by Mozart or Beethoven, for example, needs a certain attack. If a pianist carried this attack into the romantic era and played, say, Liszt's *Liebestraum* in the same spirited manner, he would get a very odd result indeed. If you have the chance, listen to Artur Rubinstein playing the *Nocturne in E flat* by Chopin. He has such a beautiful way of touching the keyboard that all the notes sound like bells, which he rings ever so gently.

You must try to learn to do this too: to caress the notes out of the flute in appropriate music; to play with a more lively, more incisive touch when the piece demands it, and never, never, on any occasion, to have a hard touch.

'The Swan' from Saint-Saëns's *Carnival of Animals* is an excellent piece for practising to get a gentle touch. Others are the 'Dance of the Blessed Spirits' from Gluck's *Orfeo*, Schumann's *Träumerei*, Debussy's *L'Après-midi* and *Syrinx*. The list, as I'm sure you'll realize, is endless.

Part Three

Lessons

There are certain things which you can teach in a book, and there are certain things which you can't teach in a book. And one of these last is music. Not that that has stopped anyone, me included. Since printing was invented, the presses have not ceased churning out advice on how to play. Laws have been laid down, rules devised, hints given, and the world has remained unchanged.

What *has* changed the world is performance, particularly in our day and age through the record industry, for the inescapable truth is that music is learned by listening to it. If this is true for the music-lover (as it clearly is: there is no such animal as a theoretical music-lover, only lovers of actual music actually played by somebody), then it is twice as true for musicians. You have to get out there into a concert hall, listen, go home, try to reproduce what you have just heard. You have to beg, borrow, steal or buy a record library and play along with the records.

A large part of musical education has to be 'teach yourself', even at the beginning, more so as you advance, because it is your own faculties of understanding and expression that are being developed – or not, as you choose. I don't mean to imply that teachers are unnecessary, a luxury to take or leave as the whim prompts. For the vast majority of us – in fact for everyone I have ever met – they are essential, and first of all as shortcuts past a deal of technical complexity. Human society is so organized that one generation is always leaning on the generation before, a system which has proved irreplaceable in the development of musical ability as in other arts and crafts. So, a teacher you will need, to introduce you to the mystery and to act as a soundingboard, critic, target-setter and encourager of your efforts. In fact, those who mean to make a career out of the flute should have, in my view, several teachers in succession. There is always another side to a question or an interpretation: fresh approaches can do only good.

In my time I have done a teaching stint or two, both of individual students and of classes. As a rule, the one-to-one relation of individual pupil to individual teacher has proved the more musically useful. In classes there is a tendency for everybody present to take to heart strictures intended only for the player currently under review. It is as if I, as first-aid attendant, advised one youngster to put a plaster on his cut finger, whereupon everyone else immediately decorates their perfectly undamaged fingers with Elastoplast. One likes to be listened to, but not so undiscriminatingly. Music is about discrimination.

Which is another reason why books don't make good teachers. They launch their message into the wide world without any chance of tailoring it to a reader's personal needs.

And now, having thoroughly depressed myself and anyone who happens to be listening with the pointlessness of writing or reading this book, I propose to say a few tentative words about the performance of some of the major areas of flute music. If I had one or other of you playing this music in class, I suspect the interruptions would be frequent, and the observations many. But, not having the opportunity for this sort of detail, I shall confine myself to general remarks. At least it can be said for them that they derive from long experience of the works in question, plus the conviction that too often these works are not played as well as they should be.

Fourteen
Playing Bach

Johann Sebastian Bach in particular is often ill served by flute players. He is a difficult composer to do justice to, for several reasons. One is quite simply his greatness. He has become a monument, not the most cheering of things to have around. People approach him with solemn respect. The results can be dreary. At the same time, just because he is the greatest, there are immense depths of meaning in his music which only a player of maturity can gauge. Thirdly, he poses technical problems. It was a trick of his to compose music not really typical of the instrument he wrote it for, without troubling about the feats he was demanding of musicians. An example is the *Partita for Solo Flute in A Minor*, which is very nicely written – for the violin. The bonus is that Bach's music is eminently transcribable. Perhaps that is what he intended: think of the music first, share it out among the instruments after-wards, and if the first flute doesn't turn up on the night, okay, hand it over to the first fiddle. As it happens, no manuscript of the *Partita* exists which in Bach's hand ascribes it to the flute (though he is believed to have written it for Buffardin). But in general Bach did not care too much about flute players when he wrote for them. He just wrote the piece, overlooked the little matter of breathing, and left the players to survive as best they could.

That said, there is no way you are going to get through life without playing Bach, and since he deserves the best, you must do your best to deserve him.

The first guideline I would suggest is not to tackle him too soon. A beginner attempting one of the major works is like a novice driver invited to try out a newly bought Rolls-Royce in the High Street on market day, a reckless proceeding, I hope you agree. Leave the big pieces till you are big, and start off with little minuets and the like.

Breathing

This has the advantage that you grow to meet the master at the same pace in understanding and interpretation as in technical accomplishment and physical capabilities such as breath-power. As I have said, Bach did not worry overmuch about the wind player's need to breathe now and again, so a first difficulty you meet in his music is the length of the phrases. There is no magical resolution to the difficulty: the phrases remain long, the lung capacity remains finite, the music requires that the lungs last out to the end of the phrase. For example, the first phrase in the *E minor Sonata* should always be played with a single breath. Therefore the stark answer is that you must learn a grown-up manner of breathing.

For purposes of comparison, here are the opening bars of the *E minor*, first with the natural breaks suitable for a not yet grown-up player, or at any rate the least offensive ones, then as you should aim one day to blow it:

Similarly with other long phrases in Bach's music, work to leave childhood behind.

Colour

A second thing you must do with these long phrases is consciously to choose the colour you want. A lot of people just pick up the flute and off they go, not caring how the sound comes out, perhaps not sure how it *will* come out, and as sadly or happily surprised as any stray listener by the unintended result. In this age of enlightenment such lack of planning is not good enough. The player must be aware of what he means to express in the music, and in consequence be able to say this particular phrase should be dark or light, sombre or happy, and play accordingly. Having covered this ground in a previous chapter, we can take it that readers have some idea of how to go about choosing the expression to match the mood.

I would just like to warn you off one small affectation, what I call the crescendo-on-the-long-note syndrome. It is as though every long note is a temptation to a crescendo. Violin players confront long notes without succumbing to the temptation, so do piano players, but flute players! We are more musical! Or are we? There is a time and place for crescendos, when and where they actually have a function. To put them in routinely, automatically, at the mere sight of a long note, is to rob the performance of meaning.

Articulation

As with colour, so with articulation you have to be choosy. In a slow movement the articulation should be soft. Compare yourself to a violinist. Like you he can start a note in various different ways. At one extreme the bow bites into the string so that the note bursts into life with a vigorous zing. At the other extreme the bow is moving before the note emerges out of nothing into audibility. The first of these extremes should be avoided in Bach's slow movements, the second should be your model.

To recapitulate: breath control, awareness of colour, and soft articulation all contribute to making a slow movement more beautiful and more serene.

The articulation of fast passages has of course to be different. Here the danger to be avoided is an overly calculated articulation which exaggerates the staccato, sticking each note out like so many exclamation marks. It is clarity of articulation we are after, not over-emphasis. Strive for a natural effect and a rounded staccato – and if you don't perfectly grasp what I mean, I don't blame you: these are subtleties to be heard, not said. But if you familiarize yourself with good performances of Bach, you will get the point fast enough.

Tempi

Playing Bach, nearly everybody to my mind does the fast movements too slow and the slow movements too fast. The result is that the true depth of the slow passages is not discovered, far less explored; whereas all the lively brilliant bits come out sounding as if someone had hard labour on his hands which he was failing to get the better of.

The thing people forget about Bach-the-monument is that he was a virtuoso. In his own day he was admired for the clever dangerous stuff on the high wire. It took posterity to muffle him in stodgy dignity. Quantz, flute player in partnership with Frederick the Great, tells a relevant tale. Quantz used to accompany old Fred on all his marches, to be on hand when music-making was required—which was usually: Frederick was King of Prussia only in his spare time. On one such journey, they came to Leipzig or somewhere, went into a church, and heard what Quantz described as the most fantastic organ playing he had ever heard. For future reference he noted the player's name, J. S. Bach, and assured his readers they would likely hear more of the same. The point we have to remember is that Bach was *glamorously* good. In addition to his superb playing of the organ he was an accomplished violin player, and his greatness as composer and general all-round musician in time attracted other top musicians, so that the people he was writing music for really knew what they were about, virtuosi to a man almost. He gave them compositions to show off their talents.

Since these are the compositions which you in turn intend to expose to the public ear, remember to inject a bit of virtuosity where appropriate. This involves playing with energy, passion and speed. After slaving all day in their insurance offices and such-like, the audience comes to a concert hoping to hear something that will thrill them to the bones. Bach meant them to be thrilled to the bones. It's up to you not to let him and the audience down. Give them the works.

That's my general advice for the lively passages. However, to be good at playing fast is not enough. You have to be good at playing slow as well, with due attention paid to breathing, colour and articulation, and a developed sense of the differences between andante, adagio, largo and so forth. Since these are not precise terms, it is a nice judgment to decide what slow and fast mean. Metronomes notwithstanding, the judgment is in the end yours, but you can give it a helping hand by comparing recorded performances and choosing from them the interpretation of tempi which best suits your own view of the piece. A word of warning: performances with orchestra are almost always compromises between visions. I myself have played slow movements more quickly than I liked, under the beat of a hustling conductor.

Fifteen
Playing Baroque Music

The works of Bach and Handel – born in the same year (1685) and dying in the same decade (1750 in Bach's case, 1759 in Handel's) – mark the ultimate development of baroque music before it gave place to the classical style of Haydn, Mozart, Gluck and company. But, although there are features in common between Bach's compositions and the earliest baroque music, dating from around 1600, there is also more than a century of development separating them. In fact it was development on all sides. For a start the very structure of our music, the major and minor keys, was worked out during this period, and the equal-tempered tuning system invented, with harmonic consequences that can't be underrated. Secondly, all the major musical forms began to take shape – opera, sonata, symphony, concerto, cantata, oratorio: you name it, its roots are in baroque. A third interesting move was that instrumental music began to equal vocal music in popular regard (in the classical era instruments would definitely outstrip voices), and a corollary of this was that new instruments were made and old ones improved. Finally, it was a time when ever increasing esteem was granted to solo and ensemble performers.

These are all good reasons for us to be grateful to baroque music, and to show our gratitude by trying to understand what it was all about. True we have a couple of legitimate grouses, too, in that, to begin with, composers wrote more for recorders than for flutes proper, and in that it was an age when the strings tended to monopolize attention. Both these wrongs were put right before baroque left the scene, however, and the flute ended up technically superior and with music to show off its new powers.

Since I have already said my brief say on Bach, I shall concentrate in this lesson on lesser lights of the baroque – not that being lesser than Bach means they were not still great composers. A roll-call including such names as Monteverdi, Lully, Scarlatti, Telemann, Vivaldi, Rameau, Couperin, Corelli and Purcell is not to be treated with anything other than respect.

The decoration of a simple melody

Baroque music set out to make a revolution, which, like other revolutions, turned out to be not such a radical break with the past as was intended. In place of the polyphony of the Renaissance, these brave new composers put the emphasis on the solo voice, the contrast of the melody with the bass line, and the expressive harmonies in between. For the solo voice of this set-up, which is what primarily concerns you and me, the essence of this music is the decoration of a simple melody.

According to taste, you could think of it as the nine hundred ways to complicate simplicity, or nine hundred beauty aids for the plain and homely. The same phenomenon is to be found in the architecture of the time (it is intriguing to note that musical styles have visual counterparts). For example, once upon a time a church was a church whose pillars and arches stood revealed without disguise. But by the time the baroquery-rockery boys had finished with it, it had roses coming out of the cracks. So with music: the melody, which may be no more complicated than a folk song, is prettied up with flowery inventions.

Hence this is very charming music to play. The folk song has definitely come up from below-stairs to meet the polite company in the drawingroom (or the 'chamber': the expression 'chamber music' dates from this time too, along with all the other new developments). The performers' duty is to keep both parts in balance. That is, the architecture of the piece as a whole must not be smothered by the fancy work, but the roses must bloom with seductive beauty.

The decoration is meant to be an elegant way of getting from one note to the next, but how precisely the journey is made is up to the performer – within reason. Baroque music is intended to have an element of improvisation in it, so that this decoration or that can be chosen according to the mood of the moment. But, as with other forms of improvised music, the improvisation in baroque is hedged securely about with rules and regulations, many concerned with the then developing harmonic system.

Aids to understanding

The essential task, then, in playing baroque music is to get to know the rules and regulations.

If you are a linguist, you could go to the horse's mouth for the explanation. There is the treatise by our old friend Quantz already mentioned in Part I, and another, also from the eighteenth century, called *L'Art de toucher le clavecin*, by Couperin. This sets out to describe all these ornaments and to show how they should be used to express the composer's intentions.

Secondly, you can turn your attention to Telemann's *Methodischen Sonaten*, an excellent illustration of the baroque approach to life. Telemann wrote out these sonatas twice over, line by line, with the melody alone on one line then – on the line underneath – the melody plus all possible ornamentation. (A page from one of them is given on pages 161–3.) I doubt he ever intended his music to be played in this somewhat cluttered fashion; he was just demonstrating the range of possibilities with typical German thoroughness.

And thirdly, you can really get into the spirit of the thing by listening to some notable practitioners on record, foremost among them perhaps Franz Brüggen. Baroque music went very completely out of fashion in the nineteenth

162

From Telemann, *Methodischen Sonaten*, sonata in G Minor

century, but of late it has come rippling back with a vengeance and is now a highly specialized field. So you won't lack for models.

I play a fair amount of it myself, and know that the fourth and essential way of getting to know this style is simply experience. Experience can be a trifle disconcerting at times. The rules don't always stay the same from country to country, even from town to town, so it's as well to polish up your ornaments if you plan to hawk this music around.

Presuming you have the rules and regulations mastered, the next thing to develop is an appreciation of how your decorated melodic line fits with the bass line. The relationship is, as I have suggested, a harmonic one. In the seventeenth and eighteenth centuries the exploration of major and minor keys and the possibility of modulating from one key to another were exciting and delightful novelties. You should try to reproduce for yourself the pleasures of harmonic discovery.

Lastly, a warning. Playing the disinterred music of the past can be intimidating, especially when the music in question carries so many rules, regulations and conventions that it takes volumes to list and explain them. The temptation is to be correct to the point of inflexibility. This temptation must be resisted. In a way it would be nice, when performing, to forget that tonight's composition was written at a certain date, in a certain country, at a certain stage of our changing culture, and simply to play it as if it were newly minted. In the case of baroque music, you do have to get inside that past world before you can make it actual to the present. But this doesn't involve presenting, say, Vivaldi's *Four Seasons* as a scholarly thesis. Whenever music was written, your attitude to it must be the same in one respect: to get the essence of what the composer put on paper into sound. Every jig should have the vitality of a Dublin street. Every sad, tender, reflective piece should carry its message to the audience whatever the musical conventions of the century in which it was written.

So, in playing baroque music, don't be afraid of expressing sentiment. Remember it was written to give pleasure, and that's what you must perform it for now.

Sixteen
Some Major Solos

In this chapter I want to talk about a few of the pieces that can't be avoided in a normal Western flute-playing career. Because they are beautiful, because they show the flute to advantage, you are sure to succumb to their temptation sooner or later, and probably sooner than you ought. The fact that none of us can resist having a bash at them may account for my impression that all too often the performance leaves something to be desired. Specifically I think that the different character of these different pieces is not always properly and profoundly understood.

As I have just said in reference to baroque, we don't want musicological scholarship to dry the juices out of music, so that what emerges from the flute sounds like illustrations to a learned treatise. But nor do we want the composer's intentions misunderstood, and it is an undeniable truth that the ideas and conventions of the composer's time are factors in his intentions. Hence, it is as well to have a feeling for the music of different periods. But that is not enough. Within the musical framework of his era, the composer is an individual with something personal to say. You must listen for this message and find ways to pass it on.

In this attempt, I would urge you not to be too literal. The limited symbols of musical notation have, I've noticed, an inhibiting effect on many young performers, who seem to believe there is some standard to be striven for – whether in interpreting a crotchet, or a pianissimo, or the speed of an allegro, or whatever. As you know, if you think about it, all these things are relative. A comparison with the written word may drive the point home. A poem may be lively and vigorous like Kipling's 'Boots', sombre and awesome like Tennyson's 'Charge of the Light Brigade', reflective and philosophical like Gray's 'Elegy in a Country Churchyard', tender and charming like any number of love poems; and many, many other things besides. But match one with another, and the words on the page look much the same. The differences of pace, rhythm, mood and meaning escape the typesetting. And so with music.

Another object lesson. Folk music has been passed down the generations by performance, without benefit of score. As a result, it has a splendid freedom – sometimes blossoming out, it must be admitted, into fistfuls of rival versions, from one village, country or continent to another. Clearly, we can't boldly dismiss the authentic texts of music known and loved for years or, as the case may be, centuries. But the notion of learning this music from performance, rather than from the printed page, may help undo a few unnecessary constraints.

Syrinx

This, if anything, is the big unavoidable standard piece that everybody has to play, the one and only flute solo Debussy ever wrote. If you happen to be ten years old, the chances are that the difficulty of the actual notes will deter you from attempting it this year and next; which is all to the good.

For the fact is that no ten-year-old, and precious few teenagers, have any conception of what *Syrinx* is all about. Debussy got his inspiration from one of those Greek fables that show the gods misbehaving in tiresomely human fashion. Pan, the god in question, was a rough fellow to look at, half goat, half man, but notwithstanding his lack of personal advantages he conceived a passion for a certain nymph, Syrinx, and so pestered her with his lustful attentions that she found escape only when she was changed into a bunch of reeds in the river. One talent Pan did have was a pretty way with music. He made a flute from the reeds she had turned into and *Syrinx* is, in fact, Pan's song to the nymph, which begins by calling for her, then wheedling and coaxing when she doesn't appear, goes on to express the erotic intensity of his desire, declaims the passion in his heart, the ache of his loneliness, and ends utterly forlorn. Quite a *tour de force* around the emotions.

I think there are commonly two faults in the way this piece is performed. First, it is too often played with detachment, which robs it of any meaning whatsoever. Presuming that the notes have been securely mastered and the technical problems dealt with, you should, in my view, play the music with greater freedom than is generally allowed. It is music to be flirted with, cajoling, pleading, protesting, persuasive music, in which every phrase must bear the right emotional charge. You can't do this by dressing up feeling in straitjackets of scrupulous tempi and the like.

My second grouse is that it is nearly always played too slowly. What I think happens is this: *Syrinx* is first tackled by youthful players who find its technical demands somewhat beyond them. Sensibly enough in the circumstances, they slow down Pan's love-song to the speed at which they can stagger through it. Time passes, technique improves, but *Syrinx* stays unspeeded up, its plaintive message to the unresponsive reeds bogged down at the tempo first thought of, all those years ago. So it loses impetus and urgency, and again the passion is ironed out of it.

Confident that I am addressing people of common sense, I know you won't go overboard on these suggestions to play more freely and quickly. It is a *trifle* more freedom which is wanted, a *little* more speed than is normally accepted. But first learn what the piece is trying to say, and then you will find the way to say it in your turn.

Dance of the Blessed Spirits

This is another cup of tea altogether. The pleasures and anguishes of the flesh don't concern us here. Here we are trying to express purer and severer emotions altogether.

It is undeniably sad music. How should one set about playing sad music? To squeeze a tear or two out of an audience may be no bad thing, but one doesn't want to send the listeners home thoroughly depressed, nor thoroughly to depress oneself. There should be no danger of your being a wet blanket with Gluck's *Dance*, for sad music (likewise sad literature), if properly presented, lifts rather than lowers the spirits, compelling an acknowledgement that there is beauty even in tragedy. This is one of a few ways in which art scores over life.

More specifically, the sadness of the *Dance of the Blessed Spirits* has in its power to move an element of hope. It has serenity and depth. It has a sort of greatness. These are the qualities you must try to find in the music, and to express when you play it. I think you can hardly have missed hearing the record of Kathleen Ferrier singing Orpheus's lament for Eurydice, from the same opera by Gluck. (And if you have not yet heard this historic recording, go and find it at once!) She found the serenity and depth with such overwhelming success that her performance of this essentially sad music has been turning up on request programmes ever since. As I have said before, and will doubtless advise again, listen to performers of Kathleen Ferrier's outstanding calibre, and do your best to reproduce their virtues.

One small technical hint: in the middle of the *Dance* there is a passage in dotted notes. Dots on notes, as we all know, mean staccato. But staccato, as we have seen, means 'separate', which is not the same thing as 'short'. These notes should of course be detached, but they should float on the air. So don't play them brisk and short and lively.

Playing with piano

Syrinx is a true solo. *The Dance of the Blessed Spirits* is accompanied by orchestra. Now I want to turn to music which is neither the one nor the other but shares characteristics in common with both. We are not thinking here about flute solos with piano accompaniment, but flute-and-piano pieces, for which you can equally read piano-and-flute pieces. Neither instrument has the edge over the other, and the music they produce is a joint statement. To illustrate the genre I propose to look at Martinu's *Sonata* and Schubert's *Theme and Variations* on 'Trockne Blumen'.

The main thing to say about such music is that each player must thoroughly know the other player's part. This may seem obvious but it is commonly ignored. It is perhaps understandable with children striving to put their first sonata together and well content if they and the piano reach the finishing line at much the same time. Unfortunately many grown-up flute players too go through life without finding out what is happening on the piano, and therefore without knowing the truth about the music they are trying to play.

In two players getting to know each other's part, the pianist has an initial advantage. The whole thing is written on the page in front of him, whereas the flute player's manuscript consists only of his single line. But the flute player must still study the other player's score, memorizing the piano part alongside his own. Memorizing one's own part is the ideal treatment for solos, sonatas and indeed any music other than the straightforward orchestral variety. It is a sign that you know what you are doing, and a necessary preliminary to thinking really hard about the piece in question so that the whole thing is put across coherently. As it happens, thoroughly knowing the piano part is a great help to memorizing your own part in this type of music because memorizing depends on landmarks which are just as likely to be given to the piano as to the flute.

Presuming both partners have taken this advice on board and got their own and the other person's notes by heart, the next stage in the business is reaching a joint interpretation. In my experience an interpretation is arrived at more in the playing than in the discussing, although there's no harm in a word of explanation here and there. But what comes first of all is listening – to your partner, of course, but also to the ideal music in your mind.

We have already spared a thought or two for the inhibiting effect of musical scores and I have urged you to loosen the bonds of scruple a little. This injunction applies as much to performance with piano as to solo performance, though naturally freedom of thought in the former case must be mutually arrived at. For example, a composer may indicate at the beginning of a movement of a sonata that it is allegro or moderato or something else again. But it is not advisable, nor yet musically sensible, to play through-out strictly in the same tempo. Very often the composer's ideas are a great deal more flexible and subtle than that first tempo instruction suggests. Very often, without any indication of change of speed, his ideas are clearly more legato, quieter in mood, or conversely have a sudden infusion of urgency or excitement. It is only doing right by the composer to hear these subtleties and slacken or speed up the tempo to suit. More particularly, when the composer introduces a new piece of material it is important not to attack it precisely in the manner handed out to the material that went before, but to think about what the change means.

With two musical sensibilities working on the problem the freedom of either one is necessarily limited. But since this sort of music is a dialogue, it is essential that you reach prior agreement about what you are going to say. The script must be in order before exposure to the public. The reading must be the product of two people, and not just somebody racing after a wild flute player with a piano part.

Consideration of the piano player is of the first import-ance for anyone attempting the Martinu *Sonata*. If you are to have any success at all, you have to have a really tremendous pianist, because the piano part is so difficult that only the best players can do it justice. Not that the flute player has an easy ride. There are three particular areas of difficulty. To begin with, the *Sonata* is a virtuoso piece, built very largely on scales, every note of which has to be exactly together with the piano if it is to sound as charming as the composer intended. Secondly, there is lavish use of syncopation which, if clumsily handled, can indeed suggest that piano and flute are at odds with each other. And thirdly, a lot of this *Sonata* is in the high register where not too many flute players are completely at their ease.

I am sure that anyone even faintly interested in music and younger than the jazz age knows what syncopation means: a deliberate off-setting of the normal rhythm so that the emphasis falls where you don't expect it. The word is related with *syncope* which – in human biology – refers to something going temporarily wrong with the circulation of the blood, bringing about a faint, swoon, or loss of consciousness. Music does not go to such drastic lengths. It messes about with the natural pulse beat only to enhance excitement, not to knock the listener out altogether, and composers have been syncopating for centuries. Undoubtedly, though, it is a favoured device of the twentieth century.

The first statement of the first movement of the *Sonata* has to be *sung*. Then suddenly the music becomes soft and pleading, with a built-in legato syncopation. To bring out the dynamic quality of this progress requires that you take care to play it to the last, least, finest degree. But the difficulties of syncopation don't really strike home until the last movement where it occurs at speed with many other things happening at the same time. Here you have not simply to *know* the piano part but to be consciously aware of it, at least when first tackling the *Sonata*. Two things must be ticking over in your head: the piano beat and your own syncopated beat. These separate rhythms should be kept in mind until the point comes where you can forget the mechanics, forget the piano part, and just happily put the whole thing together as the composer envisaged it.

So much for the syncopation. The problem of playing at the highest reaches of the flute's register tends to get neglected for the mutually supporting reasons that it is difficult to do and not much used. But, as I have emphasized before, everything you do should be beautiful. There must be elegance in every note from top to bottom and back again. If, along with a lot of other people, you have hitherto shunned hard work on the high notes, it is certainly inadvisable to make the Martinu *Sonata* your first venture in beating the problem. The preparations for eventually coming to grips with the *Sonata* can, however, start now, with long tone exercises going up the flute instead of down, the tones managing to be soft and expressive even at the uttermost limit. This is not easy, but neither is it impossible to achieve.

Bohuslav Martinu wrote the *Sonata* for George Laurent, who was solo flute for the Boston Symphony Orchestra, just after the Second World War. At that time Martinu was living in New England, a fact which left its mark on the music in the call of the whippoorwill, incorporated into the middle of the last movement. Do not of course let this detail suggest that here we have to do with scenic effects, a sort of nature-notes in sound. The *Sonata* is music of very high stature indeed.

The slow movement in particular is one of the most beautiful movements I have ever heard. It is like a prayer in music which comes so close to the truth about the universe that any intervention of the player's personality risks getting in the way of the message. When playing it you must strive for an honesty and a humility which so efface the self that only a vehicle for the notes survives. There exist types of music which absolutely require an assertion of the personality of the performer. The slow movement is not one such. You have to keep in the background, looking for the stillness at its heart.

To come back to earth, the slow movement presents a little technical problem of its own, not unconnected with its prayerful character. This is the by now well rehearsed problem of having enough breath to encompass the phrases. Once again, we have here a piece of music in which, when it is first attempted in youth, a number of breath marks cannot be dispensed with; and once again, too often people fail to remove some of them as they grow up. I think they get used to hearing it as they first did it. It sounds right to them and somehow blocks their vision of how it could be improved. Let me urge you, as you get older, to make the transition from musical childhood to musical adulthood, if such an expression is permitted.

The *Sonata* – the last movement this time – illustrates another of my hobby-horses. A lot of staccato notes occur which, as I've said so often in the past, are not necessarily short, but detached. To get some sense out of the first statement in this movement, you have to be careful not to play the notes too short but see that they have a ring to them.

Earlier I mentioned scales. Not only in the *Sonata*, but frequently elsewhere in Martinu's compositions they are the infrastructure. It so happens that much of his early youth was spent with his family up a tower, as his dad was a fireman, so that for a number of years it was all up and down for young Bohuslav! I fancy this biographical circumstance shows in the music. So many scale passages slowly descend as if he was climbing down the ladder to get his feet on solid ground at last.

The big snag about Schubert's *Theme and Variations* is the intonation. This piece is notorious for the difficulty of the intonation for the simple reason that it is in E minor, and, as you have probably already discovered, E♮ is not so good anywhere along the flute. The usual tendency is that the low E is too low, the middle one is somewhere else again, and the top one is sharp. Problems of intonation become critical in the *Theme and Variations* at moments when, after some bars of piano, the flute comes in again and, if the audience's combined teeth are not to be put on edge, must come in at precisely the same pitch.

Of course this piece does not have a monopoly of the

problem, which is something that orchestral musicians, for example, encounter all the time. Some of their solutions are pretty forthright. The oboe player Lothar Koch, whom I used to play alongside in the Berlin Philharmonic, used simply to test the note quite loud before coming in, and his pitch, when he did start to play, always sounded right. In orchestral music part of the art of playing in tune is to continue at the same pitch as the person before, even if his pitch was wrong. Then you adjust as you go along to arrive at the pitch you feel to be right.

Things are not quite the same when all that is in question is you and a piano and Schubert. The piano's pitch can be expected to remain constant, it is up to the flute to be on centre, and in the circumstances the player cannot copy Lothar Koch and give a perfectly audible try-out toot. However, the piano does provide cover for some more furtive experiment. I often test the note I am about to play by the gentlest of breaths, well below the audience's hearing threshold, and so I know whether to sharpen it by turning the flute out, or to flatten it by turning it in.

Intonation apart, the *Theme and Variations* demands a thorough mastery of the flute to put over all its riches. It offers the skilful flute player plenty of occasion for enjoyment and display and a whole range of emotions to express. My own preference is to play it through all seven variations without, as far as possible, stopping. But there is one stop that I do acknowledge to be necessary. The Fifth Variation is such a blast for the flute that I think one just has to have a moment to wipe the sweat off one's brow and gather one's forces to continue.

But in the general cause of coming out alive at the end, I usually leave out some of the repeats that Schubert indicated. I do all the repeats in the Theme and then none until the slow movement, Variation 3. When eight bars are repeated, and repeated, and repeated, it becomes very difficult to impart a *nuance*, and the audience tends to get a bit glassy-eyed under the insistence of all this repetition. With some repeats cut out, such misfortunes are avoided and as a result of this the piece is much more compact.

Contriving not to sound always the same is a challenge which meets the player right from the start, in the Introduction. In fact, being an introduction to a whole lot of material it naturally has a great many ideas and statements and expressions in it, some distant and reflective, others very positive, virtuoso and brilliant. Clearly a range of treatment is needed. I would suggest you pay attention to two things in particular.

First, the speed. Most commonly this introduction is played too slowly, by performers probing so deeply for the message that they miss half of it and fail to see the wood for the trees. A good speed, then, is the first requirement, but it must be one which is easily adjustable, able to take account of those statements which are more forward going as well as of those which hold back a little bit. In particular, just the end of the Introduction, before the Theme, there is a sort of little cadenza, which is not recognized as such by many players. Since it is printed as part of the ongoing tune, they overlook its real nature and play it in strict tempo. I have the feeling that the tempo should be a little quicker here to give this cadenza a natural flow, leading into the melody which comes first on the piano.

Secondly, you have to be very careful about the colour of the tone. It is advisable to use as many different colours as possible, in order to express the variety of Schubert's ideas in this Introduction, and to convince the listener that it is not just a music box grinding thoughtlessly along, but actually has a range of things to say.

Of course these words of advice – on studying speed and colouring in light of the material – apply to the whole composition through all its variations. But the different character of the variations is readily appreciated. Only the musically backward would consider playing them in the same way. My point is that such flexibility must be brought to the Introduction too.

The other points I have to make can be quickly despatched. To begin with, the First Variation, like the

Introduction, should not be taken too slowly. It looks frighteningly black on paper, but, with a little bit of practice you can get it going at a fairly reasonable speed.

The slow movement, Variation 3, deserves a measure of special attention. Rarely have I heard a performance where I really accepted what the flute player was doing. My own practice is to conjure up in my head, before I play this movement, the sound of Dietrich Fischer-Dieskau singing Schubert. It is remarkable how he bends the music around to give it meaning. Study a Schubert record of his and base your performance of the slow movement on that.

And now, at last, a word of comfort for the staccato experts whom I am constantly holding back. The *Theme and Variations* gives you your chance to be as short as you can contrive in the Sixth Variation. But, for it to be effective, you need a good piano player who can play staccato softly.

At the end of the penultimate variation, I take the liberty of improving on Schubert by altering a note, pushing it an octave higher. Where he wrote:

I play:

One of my students suggested this dodge to me one day and, as I am an adopter of good ideas, I adopted it immediately. For starters, you can actually hear the revised version note, whereas the B♮ of Schubert's choice really gets lost in the clamour, and secondly, it sounds better together with the piano.

I like to begin the last Variation very softly, with the

notes a trifle on the short side, then, in the next eight bars, play a little longer and louder. This Variation is a march, and when I am performing it I always envisage a little band, first heard when it is still off-stage, then growing loud and clear as it comes into view.

The Coda is one of Schubert's most brilliant moments, so, to celebrate it, I really step on the gas and put the music in top gear. Nor do I let it slacken as we come into the finish. There is a tendency for people to make rallentandos at certain musical junctures as a matter of form, whether they believe in the rallentando or not, or could justify it if challenged. Not for me, not here. Sometimes to go straight to the end without slowing up and go absolutely bang on the last chord is the most thrilling thing you can possibly do.

People say the repertoire for the solo flute is limited and if comparisons are made with music written for some other musical instruments, there is not one of us that can deny the charge. In these lessons the limited repertoire has necessarily been restricted even further but I hope that I have touched on a few items and areas of interest, and, in relating how I personally prepare some pieces for performance, I also hope to spur reflection and ambition in at least some apprentice players.

For myself, the solo flute repertoire – which, of course, I play and replay all the time – never wears out its charms, never seems restricting or threadbare or over-familiar. The reason is that each time a piece is played, it involves the rebirth of an individual – me. Today I am a different James Galway from the one I was yesterday, and I trust I shall be another one tomorrow. Naturally all these different individuals see the music with fresh eyes and even, on occasion, disagree with some detail of emphasis or tempo which satisfied their predecessors. There is no danger whatever of me or anybody else having the last word on the subject. Music of this quality offers infinite possibilities for discovery.

Seventeen
Listening to Records

Just to remind you: nobody ever became a great musician by reading a book. All great musicians got that way by listening to music, playing music, and talking music with fellow musicians, plus some help from genetic inheritance and a lot of hard work. And in our day and age the first of these factors has been made ridiculously easy by two inventions, broadcasting and recording. What you do with your transistor, I leave to you, in order to concentrate in this chapter on urging you to make the most of records or cassettes.

The gramophone as teacher

The gramophone as teacher, as well as source of enjoyment, is something I have long known about from experience. From the first day my family had one, the gramophone played a very important part in my life, although the gramophone in question was the wind-up sort now found only in museums, and our records totalled at that point only two. On one Fritz Kreisler played some of the encores he had composed to delight concert audiences. The other was Al Jolson singing *Mammy*, with which my brother and I would sing along, having no idea of the real sentiment behind it, but just for the laugh. These two records got worn almost smooth, in the course of which operation I acquired an admiration for Kreisler's violin playing which has never faded.

It was some years before we could afford an electric gramophone, but fortunately there were neighbours. When I got into playing the flute, I used regularly to inflict my company on a lady down the street, who thought it great to have a kid come in to listen to Mozart in her little front room. Among this lady's store of records were quite a few by flute players, and it was then I began to realize that I could learn a lot. Naturally I tried to imitate them, and whereas nobody could explain in words how Mozart could, should or might be played, here were models to be listened to. You can talk all you want about music, but if you can't hear and can't pick up the message through hearing, you might as well give up.

Later I had a girl friend whose family possessed a gramophone and a stack of records, among which I particularly remember the Brandenburgs and the Beethoven Violin Concerto played by Yehudi Menuhin. I used to hang out with her and play these records over and over, so that the music really stuck in my head. So the repertoire – not of what I played, but of what I was beginning to know – grew wider. I never listened to pop music, once I got mesmerized with the classical variety.

As I grew up, my gramophone listening got more specialized, as it were. My teacher in London, John Francis, had a great gramophone, plus the recordings of Marcel Moyse, to this day my hero on the flute. In addition, I would listen to orchestral symphonies with the express purpose of discovering how the flute players in this or that orchestra performed. Apart from saving you the trouble of hassling with public transport on the way to a concert on a cold wet night, the recording gives you the chance to hear it through a second time, if you wish, or, if you wish, to hear one bar five times. Not that there's anything to equal the excitement of a live concert, but for a study of a piece or a performance, the record is the thing. I can't recommend too highly that anybody who wants to play an instrument gets a load of records by a good exponent of that instrument and just takes a bath in the sound of it.

Comparing flute players

Maybe I should not name names of good exponents of the flute, but on the understanding that these are just random suggestions, hardly an exhaustive list, I shall risk it. From France there is Jean-Pierre Rampal, from England William Bennett and from America quite a number, Julius Baker being among the most notable.

Through listening to players of this stature, you will get to know the best of the different schools. It is a good idea to contrast two or more players' performances of the same piece. Maybe one of them has a more brilliant approach, another a more soulful one, while the third has qualities altogether different from the first two. To note such varying excellences among the best players in the world is a very helpful exercise. I always think it is a little bit dangerous to get so stuck on one teacher (or in this case, one model) that you reject counsel from any other source, like the fundamentalist Christian who simply denies that Buddha has any wisdom to impart at all. Better to pick and choose from the best of any school of thought, or of flute playing.

Now the piece of advice I have just handed out sounds as if it was meant for millionaires. As you can guess from the personal digression above, on the gramophones of my youth, I am well aware of the problems of affording one recording of a piece, never mind two or three. But there are such things as libraries, and, as you become more committed, there are parents, relatives, birthday presents and record tokens to be exploited. Instead of doubling up on recordings of the same piece by different players, you could trim the cost and still make the comparison of styles by buying this fellow playing Mozart and the other playing Bach. You would also be well advised to accept the guidance of a teacher as to which records to purchase in the first place. What you may not do is turn a deaf ear to this marvellous source of instruction in the technique of the flute and the interpretation of music.

Beyond the flute

Don't stop at flutes. No matter how young a child is, he or she should listen to other instrumentalists and to singers.

I know this is hard advice to take. Children, my own included, tend to have such obsessional, blinkered enthusiasms that any distraction from the matter at issue is resisted until the enthusiasm is worked out of the system. But for two good reasons, it is wise not to be so blinkered that you listen only to flute music. One is that flutes are played in ensembles and orchestras, so, if you are ever called on to play in such contexts, it helps to have an appreciation of other sorts of instrument. The second and more important reason is that musical expression has many voices, and the more of them you learn to respond to, the more of an all-round musician you will ultimately be. For myself, there is a trio of soloists (if you get my meaning) whom I constantly replay: Heifetz on violin, Horowitz on piano, and Maria Callas. In Callas's singing there are so many colours and expressions that can't be got on a flute, such depth of quality, such quality of drama and intensity. We must all listen to tremendous musicians like her to understand what a standard of perfection is.

Learning to discriminate is what this is all about. I mean, millions of people have record players nowadays, and will spin a disc at the drop of a hat. But most of the time most of us don't really listen. The sound washes around while our minds are on other things. A fair degree of attention is needed, if you are to train your faculties of discrimination and appreciation, but even under unpromising conditions attention is possible. A friend of mine, who is so far into opera that he is a bit of a freak on it now, acquired his musical education from a cassette recorder in his car on trips back and forth to work. He began with Brahms's piano concertos, didn't really understand them at first, but persisted and advanced until now he takes arias for breakfast. He used his time in the car to develop himself, and learned, as we all can do, that understanding music is a lot more enjoyable than just listening to it as a gin-and-tonic background.

Records give us a choice. We don't have to put up with low standards. There are rival performances of this and that well-loved piece, so finely balanced, so equally excellent, that choice is very difficult indeed, even after hearing them. This is where the record library, or the understanding friend, comes in. Buy one version, borrow the other, and enjoy both.

One last word: if your teacher happens to have made a recording or two, it would be diplomatic to add them to your collection, whatever the cost.

Part Four

On Being a Flute Player

Not everyone who starts learning to play the flute is going to end up making a living out of it. Given the great number of applicants for the small number of jobs, it's just as well that there is a certain fallout along the way, although at a cost, I know, of some sore hearts and disappointed ambitions. If you, dear individual reader, hope one day to be paid for playing the flute, my advice to you is: be realistic, and in the first place be realistic about your own competence. The judgment of indulgent friends and relations is no guide in this matter. Too often kids are encouraged by the community who marvel at their cute little local flute player, all unaware that outside in the world there is a whole bunch of sharks ready to eat him or her alive.

Later in these pages I will suggest ways of (a) deciding whether you are up to the competitive demands, and (b) making the most of your talents so that they carry you into paid employment. But for the moment I would like to urge that the failure to become a professional doesn't mean the end of the flute. One of my former students is a lawyer, and she still plays the flute. Another is a nurse and likewise still gets a lot of enjoyment out of the flute between patients. Moreover, because music is very flexible, it is always possible to channel one's resources into aspects of it other than performance, aspects such as becoming a producer, or recording engineer, orchestral manager and so forth. There are many things to be done, many different paths to be taken, from the starting point of a knowledge of the flute.

On being a flute player

However, in the succeeding chapters attention will be focused on flute players who do contrive to make a career out of their instrument. As you will see, the ground covered can be strange and various, but we shall start with the obvious and straightforward way to a pay packet, the orchestra.

Eighteen
The Orchestra

Among the orchestral musicians of my acquaintance there are no millionaires, but in general they have a roof over their heads and a car, and they manage to keep their families fed, clothed and shod, and send their children to school. So, from a financial point of view, they seem to do all right. But more to the point, or at any rate as much to the point: they can have a great life if they set about things in the right way. Few enjoyments surpass playing well with good colleagues in a good orchestra, where words don't matter and music is a language used every day between individuals to express themselves as a whole. It is a very exciting and fulfilling experience. Remember, by way of contrast, that other people earn a salary for the doubtful privilege of being buried in an insurance company for a week at a time.

The problem is, find the orchestra. At present they are not so thick on the ground, and even the larger ones probably employ only three flute players, while the smaller ones usually make do with two. A new young player trying to break into this merry band of brothers needs, therefore, a plan of campaign. The first moves in it start when the said player is still at college.

Styles of different orchestras

To study the styles of the different orchestras, one of which may one day offer you a job, is an essential piece of market research. How can you give satisfaction if you don't know what the customers want? By doing a regular stint of listening to music on record, you will already have discovered that orchestras have a personality and a sound that distinguish them from one another. They get that way by choice, not by accident, so it behoves an intending recruit to take account of the preferred style.

Even orchestras of equal excellence span a spectrum with technical brilliance at one end and musical expressiveness at the other. An example of the technically brilliant variety is the Chicago Symphony Orchestra. All the players possess technical proficiency to a high degree, and every piece they play is worked out, calculated, organized. With quick, brilliant music – something tricky by Berlioz, say – the Chicago Symphony sounds absolutely phenomenal. Compare this with the Berlin Philharmonic doing (say) a Bruckner symphony. The musicians in the pay of the Berlin Philharmonic are no less proficient, but what is striking is that they all seem to know exactly which note to make longer or shorter. The phrasing is so beautiful as a whole, the orchestra bringing it off together as if one intelligence and one interpretation dictated it. And so it does, for the players are so used to working together, and so used to having the same conductor for twenty years at a stretch, that they have all come to live on the same wavelength.

More specifically, style affects the woodwind section, and flute playing in particular. For example, in the Vienna Philharmonic, the woodwind do not use vibrato. All the notes come out absolutely clear. In France and England, on the other hand, everybody uses vibrato, and in America, most do.

Quite apart from the question of vibrato, there are, as it were, national fashions in flute playing. In France it is soft and charming, in Germany more academic, in America very organized, and in England a big mixture of everything. If there is an English school nobody to my knowledge has put their finger on it yet, and the tendency is for flute playing to vary from one orchestra to the next. Which could be to your advantage. The Japanese, who know how to pick and choose imports from the West, have more or less copied the French style and injected a bit of American organization into it.

You have to study these different styles, and try and play in the manner of the group with which you hope to integrate. However, since your first employment may well not be very far afield, perhaps you could begin by concentrating on orchestras at home.

The main thing to do is actually go to their concerts, the next, to get to know the players who are going to be (you hope) your future professional colleagues. In the plan of campaign now being worked out, it is very helpful to have friends at court.

Technical proficiency

One thing there can be no doubt about is the necessity of your being able to do the job. As well as mastery of the instrument and of scales, arpeggios and so forth, this means your familiarizing yourself, before you join an orchestra, with the repertoire.

In brief (but don't take this as anywhere near complete) the repertoire includes: all the named Haydn symphonies, Mozart's last three symphonies, all the symphonies by Beethoven, Brahms and Tchaikovsky, Mahler's major works, the main operas by Mozart, Puccini and Verdi, and the big oratorios such as the *Passions* of Bach. These things, as a minimum, you have to *know*.

To get to know them involves more than studying the scores and practising the flute bits. It involves having a conception of how these works sound. Therefore you must go to concerts and listen with a receptive, critical ear. People who want to become musicians should be committed to what they are doing, committed at least to the length of regularly attending concerts of the music they hope one day to play to the public.

There are some people who are very good at sight-reading; but skilful sight-reading, although an extremely useful talent on occasion, is not a substitute for knowing the repertoire. The danger of depending on this facility is a certain mechanical, routine performance of the notes without any infusion of the feeling the composer meant to express; like an expert shorthand-typist translating dots and squiggles into English prose with never a care for what it actually means. That is not good enough. You must know your instrument, you must know your individual part, and you must also know how the music sounds as a whole. Only then will you play it with involvement.

How to audition

Presuming you have got yourself into good flute-playing trim, and done your preliminary reconnaissance of the target, now comes the crunch, the moment of engagement.

If never before experienced, this can be a little bewildering, so I shall first sketch out what sort of a set-up you can expect to find. Circumstances vary, of course, from one orchestra to another, and no generalization will cover every particular variation, but a rough idea of what confronts you is better than none.

At the minimum the people doing the audition will include the conductor, the first flute player, some other principals, and some members of the board of directors, perhaps a dozen in all. In Germany, however, where they have a democratic voting system, the whole orchestra may sit in judgment on the new recruits.

Most orchestras announce beforehand what the audition pieces will be. You simply apply and are sent a list, which typically might include the *Symphony No. 4*, by Brahms, *Till Eulenspiegel*, *L'Après-midi d'un faune*, *Daphnis and Chloë*, *Sinfonia Domestica*, maybe a piece from a Strauss opera – things with testing passages for the flute. The idea of an orchestral audition is not to test your abilities on – say – an early Haydn symphony, but to see how you sound in the tricky bits, when the chips are down, or when the flute has the starring role. The best organized outfits are even prepared to send photocopies of the particular parts they want played. If the orchestra you are aiming to join is too disorganized to provide this service, you can only rely on your common sense and knowledge of the repertoire and practise the obvious pieces for the audition.

A popular, but in my view misguided, practice nowadays is to hold auditions behind a screen. The argument is that if the judges can't see whom they are judging, the audition won't be fixed, and the one who gets the job will do so by virtue of his skill and musicality alone. I disagree with this for several reasons, and primarily because the screen or curtain or whatever tends to blur the clarity of the sound, reducing all contestants to the same level. Everybody sounds the same behind a closed door, everybody sounds good in the next room.

But I also think the hidden-player method of audition is stupid because it fails to take account of the real world. In a sense all auditions are fixed, precisely because there is such a thing as a flute players' fraternity, and musicians already in the orchestra know very well whom among up and coming aspirants they prefer. You can make this circumstance work in your favour. Having studied the style of the orchestra in general, the applicant for a job should specifically study how the first flute plays. To improve your acquaintance with both him and his playing, you would be wise to try and wangle a few lessons from him, which may prompt him to argue in your favour at the audition, on the grounds that he knows and likes your playing and believes you are up to the job. The opinion of the expert generally has a powerful effect on others present.

In the usual course of things, anybody interested in getting a job in an orchestra will already be moving in orchestral circles. This just happens normally, as a result of one's overriding interest in life. If it is not happening in your case, try to make it happen. If you hang out with these people, they come to know you, and when an extra flute or two is needed for some special performance, they turn to the people they know. Friends – as I have suggested

– are an invaluable card to have in your hand when applying for a full-time position.

For the dismal truth about auditions is that it is sometimes very difficult to get one. The absolutely unknown player is often rejected even from this preliminary competition, and to overcome this first hurdle, a personal recommendation is the most effective boost you can have. A letter from your teacher may not be enough. A word on your behalf from somebody already in the orchestra is a good deal more persuasive. It was in this fashion that I got my first job. I was studying in Paris at the time, and my pal William Bennett was playing in the Sadlers Wells Opera Orchestra. A second flute was needed. William did two things. He advised me to come over to London to try my luck, and, more importantly, he advised the orchestra to include me among the other candidates.

Some places there are no limits on the numbers accepted for audition. In one orchestra in America in search of a flute player, the situation got so out of hand that just listening to the first round, before the short list was even drawn up, took a whole week. This overkill may have been fair to the United Nations, but it made nonsense of the audition, for how can one judge – or even keep distinct in the mind – the performance of perhaps 187 separate musicians across the span of a week? What resulted from that orchestra's blanket coverage audition was precisely what results in more selective auditions: failing the discovery of a genius, the local man was chosen.

The local man is nearly always chosen, for the reasons already outlined. He is known to the flute section, his playing has been heard, he is trusted. Hence the lesson: be the local, known, trusted person. That way you get a helping hand to the audition in the first place, and from the audition to the job.

Let us suppose you have been accepted for audition and have the required music ready. The procedure, as with beauty contests and other competitions, is of gradual elimination until the supposedly best candidate, and the one thought to be most musically and socially compatible, is isolated from the rest and offered a contract. It is unlikely that a candidate will be asked to play all the music named beforehand, and the worse his performance, the less playing will be required of him.

At least, the worst performers get kicked out straight away in sensibly run auditions. But not all auditions are sensibly run. I heard of a competition (not in fact an audition) where the adjudicators were two eminent authorities on the flute, a Frenchman and a German, whose names would be familiar to you, were I to reveal them; which I won't. These two were arguing over a player who should not have been there at all. For nerves or some other reason he could not get the competition piece started. The Frenchman was all for dismissing him pronto and passing on to the next competitor.

'No,' said the German, 'He's got twenty minutes like everybody else.'

'But it's ridiculous!'

'As it happens, he's a student of mine.'

'Ah ha!' the Frenchman said, 'So that's why you inflict twenty minutes on us!'

'Well, no,' returned his colleague. 'He's also the first flute in the local police band.'

I suppose he was thinking of possible future parking tickets. Auditions can be equally bizarre.

Bizarre or not, they must be taken seriously, and this means among other things that candidates must be in good form. Therefore, don't drink. Don't even drink the day before. A lot of us are nervous when facing this challenge which will either open the door to a career or close that door with apparent finality in our faces. Since so much hangs on it, apprehension is normal, but believe me alcohol does not help. In fact it harms. It completely wrecks any sort of technical ability you may have acquired, it clouds the head, it takes the edge off fantasy.

In case you think this is a singular judgment of my own, let me tell you a little story. Once in Paris not so long ago,

On being a flute player

I was giving a week of concerts, playing at the same time every evening, and on the wagon all day in preparation. One day I had lunch with Artur Rubinstein, who remarked that I wasn't drinking anything. Yes, says I, I have a concert tonight. 'You are very wise, Mr Galway,' he responded. 'Alcohol goes straight to the fingers.' I take it you all admire Rubinstein and trust the experience of his ninety years and believe he knows what he is talking about.

It has to be admitted that the common preference for the local man can be a disadvantage, if through circumstances beyond your control and for no fault of your own you simply cannot become that much sought after person. To people who are not selected in an audition I would say just this: don't be disheartened, don't think you have failed, don't even conclude that you played badly. Very possibly you played better than the one who got the job. You may feel that this is a very unjust state of affairs, but in the professional world a competent performance is only one of several things taken into account at an audition. Beginners in all trades and at all times discover the store set by experience. So with flute players. The experienced fellow who will fit in quickly may well be preferred to the brilliant youngster who, never having played in an orchestra, will need training.

Beginners very often find themselves outside an aggravating closed circle: to get a job you need experience, but to get experience you need a job. However, the circle is not quite so impossibly closed as it looks, and with perseverance a good player will crack a way into it. Therefore, if the first audition leaves you jobless, do not be discouraged, but try again a time or two, concentrating for best results on your own neighbourhood where everybody knows you.

In short, an unsuccessful audition is neither a disgrace nor a guarantee of life on the dole. I suggest you do a number of them before considering alternative action.

But a consistent record of failure ought to make you think again. After the ninth or tenth disappointment, it is time to question whether you are professionally up to standard, whether the orchestra is really where you belong, whether indeed the flute offers you a livelihood.

Playing in an orchestra

I would hate to be considered a member of the working classes. To me, music is not a way to earn a living but an expression of the perfection of being. What is more, I enjoy playing the flute. I believe there is absolutely no point in being shackled to it for a lifetime unless not only *I* enjoy playing it, but the listener enjoys hearing it. Music has to be what you want to do, something which makes you and everybody listening feel they are in touch with the extra-special.

I am not alone in this view. One evening in Switzerland I was sitting over a chess game with a friend of mine who teaches classical saxophone in a conservatory there. A phone call came through for him from the father of one of his pupils, asking advice on music for his son. 'Nothing too serious,' he said. 'I just want to buy something easy he can play, because he only does it for fun.' My friend is the blunt spoken sort. 'Listen,' he answered, 'The way your kid plays saxophone, it couldn't possibly be fun, not for him and not for anybody else. Why don't you tell him to practise so that it *will* be fun?' Flute playing is like other sorts of human endeavour: if you don't get involved in it totally and do the best you can, it will not be fun, it will only be boring, for you and for the person on the other end.

This warning applies to all sorts of flute playing, but I include it in the current section deliberately. A lot of people get into orchestras and die a spiritual death. When they are young, they make a supreme effort, practising until flutes are coming out of their ears, and eventually they land a job. Then, like the sportsman who achieves his four-minute mile and rests on his laurels, they stop trying to improve. To their disappointment they find the orchestra can be a bit like a factory. People go in every day, life becomes a matter of routine, commitment leaks away, and they sink to expecting no more than competence from themselves. Believe me, nothing sounds worse than an orchestra of dull, routine type players.

The dull players are the ones who find it a chore, who take no pleasure in it any more, who are disappointed in their professional and personal lives. It's hard to stick around any orchestra which has more than a few such miseries in it.

At the other end of the scale there is another threat to orchestral harmony, equally depressing to have to play alongside. This is the ego-tripper, the person who thinks he should never be in an orchestra anyway, but as he is, he's going to be the star of it. Newcomers determined to make their mark in the profession may be specially at fault here. Their attitude immediately sets up antagonisms between them and the established players and generally wrecks the relationship with the rest of the band. Again, it shows – or rather sounds. You can hear when an orchestra is happy. It is wrong, and moreover it is wrong-headed, to learn a musical instrument with a view to furthering one's ego, to being the star of an orchestra or a great big soloist or whatever. Musical instruments are learned to give pleasure to people.

So much for the negative side. There are two positive lessons to be drawn.

First, fight off routine dullness by making yourself regard every day as a new day, and every experience as a fresh one. Just as if each day was in fact the first, ask yourself, is this the best I can do? Can I play a bit softer here, a bit louder there? Can we get this passage better together? To enjoy yourself properly in an orchestra, you have to keep practising, you have to keep your morale up, and you have to make a new beginning every morning.

Second, resist the temptations of stardom, bury your ego and become part of the team. This doesn't involve declining into a mindless cog in somebody else's interpretation.

Every instrument has its voice and each voice is equally important. You will have your say, your moments to shine in, without throwing your weight about and annoying all your colleagues.

Team spirit, than which few things are more valuable to an orchestra, is something which you can contribute towards but scarcely control. As the new boy, all you can do is hope to find team spirit prevailing, and try to uphold it. Some orchestras are more rigid than others. The Berlin Philharmonic, for example, is a very highly integrated team, and when you join, you do it their way, until you find a method of expressing your own personality within the framework of the team. In other, nameless orchestras of my experience, the team spirit comes to grief on factions among the players. And, at the opposite end of the spectrum to the Berlin Philharmonic, is the session orchestra, mustered from all over the place for a one-off event like a recording. Naturally teams, team spirit and integration don't apply to them, but neither, in the circumstances, are they important.

So how can one do one's bit to foster team spirit? In the general course of orchestral life, it is useful if the players are on speaking terms. When people stop talking to each other, the collapse of the system is signalled. It means that they play in spite of, rather than with, each other. It is better to agree to disagree than to disagree in smouldering silence.

Technically the main responsibility for integration falls on the section leaders, in our case the first flute. It is his job to organize you and his other underlings, if any, both for flute performance and for fitting in with the strings and so forth. Ideally there should be no boss as such. An orchestra should be democratically run. Musical ideas should be accepted from any quarter. But the group without a good principal to rely on feels weak and leaderless.

Principles apart, there are things you can do yourself, and first try to become yet more master of the style of the orchestra you now belong to. After a few rehearsals it is possible to be something of an expert. As well as absorbing the overall style of the whole team, you learn, for instance, that the first oboe plays in such a way, and that to fit in with him you must play in that certain way too.

Oboes and oboists loom large in a flute player's career, and since the first flute sits beside the first oboe, they make a big contribution to team spirit if they work in harmony. Intonation is often a problem. The pitch of one instrument is frequently fractionally higher or lower than that of the other. So it is wise to get to know each other's sharps and flats and organize adjustments accordingly. When I was at the Royal Philharmonic, the oboe player Derek Wickens and I would have a session before a concert to check one another's intonation. This has to be done in a way which doesn't cause personal animosity, which can be a big problem with musicians: they get mortally offended if you tell them they are playing out of tune. But Derek and I did it tactfully and stayed friends, and were in tune in both meanings of the phrase. The willingness to bend a note to accommodate your neighbour is one thing that makes for a good orchestral team.

Similarly with dynamics. For example, it is very hard to play low notes softly on the oboe. The kind, generous flute player, who has the team spirit notion on board, realizes that if he plays softly, the oboe sticks out a mile. Therefore he contrives to play louder himself, in order that flute and oboe together sound like a unit with the same general designs in mind.

Where, in this brotherly scene, does the conductor fit? In the case of a resident conductor who has been there for a certain stretch of time, the chances are that he has imposed his views, both by force of character and by selection of players. Orchestral style is generally determined in the first place by conductors. So, for example, the Cleveland under George Szell, a real technician, had a sort of machine-tooled perfection in contrast to the greater freedom allowed within a framework by Herbert

von Karajan. But not all conductors have powerful personalities, and when one of this lesser breed comes as visiting
conductor to a really integrated outfit and tries to have his
way with it, he usually fails and just has to let it have its
head.

I think I am safe in saying that they don't make
conductors like they used to. In the 1930s Berlin, with such
men as Furtwängler, Bruno Walter, Klemperer as a young
man, Toscanini coming and going, or London, with Sir
Thomas Beecham and Sir Malcolm Sargent, had real
personalities, social as well as musical, in charge of
concerts. These fellows got their remarks and cartoons
about them into the daily newspapers. They also got the
respect of the orchestras under their command, and the
respect was generally mutual. Sir Thomas made sure of it
when he put his famous Royal Philharmonic together,
choosing players of great distinction such as Jack Brymer
(clarinet), my former teacher Geoffrey Gilbert (flute),
Gwydion Brook (bassoon) and Terence MacDonough
(oboe). When Beecham died and the Royal Philharmonic
was discussing a successor, MacDonough, so the story
goes, declared that he didn't care who was engaged, he
was going to continue playing for Sir Thomas. Which only
goes to show that the run-of-the-mill conductor has
problems in trying to wear a great man's shoes, and first of
all problems with some big war horse of an orchestra which
simply takes over the performance.

You can soon tell whether the conductor is in command.
It's a question of whether he knows what he wants or not.
Probably the piece being rehearsed has been played many
times before and a conception of it has sunk into the
orchestral subconscious. The fledgling conductor lets it rip
for a while, then says, 'Perhaps we should try such and
such a thing,' and if that doesn't satisfy, suggests another
little experiment. A good conductor arrives at rehearsal
with his mind made up and explains beforehand what effect
he is after. He may stop the orchestra and make it repeat
a chord or a phrase, not to discover how it sounds six

different ways, but simply to realize his vision in performance. That is true musical direction. It's a bit like setting a table for a dinner party. The expert home entertainer has the blueprint ready, the not-so-expert tries the decorations this way and that and swaps around the place settings, and generally wastes time attempting to find out what looks nice.

To have a strong conductor directing the orchestra does not rob players of the chance to make a musical innovation on their own account. Say you get a good notion, you just incorporate it in your performance at rehearsal, and if the conductor fancies it, he will accept it, and otherwise cancel the operation. This has occurred in my experience a time or two. In the slow movement of Beethoven's *Fourth Symphony* there is a scale in E♭ marked *piano*, then *pianissimo*, which demands an adjustment of the lips. Because of this technical problem it was customary to make a little pause to change the embouchure and come in *pianissimo* as Beethoven demanded. To stop on the leading note before going into the tonic seemed to me a thoroughly unnatural thing to do, and since I *could* do it without the pause, I *did* do it without the pause, one day at a rehearsal in Berlin. Von Karajan liked it well enough to ask me to repeat it, and it stayed in the performance thereafter, with me thinking, well, there goes one piece of German tradition down the drain.

So there are occasions when you can get your own way without discussing it with the conductor. Other times a conductor may call you into his room to discuss some important flute work before rehearsal, in the cause of saving time. But it's the playing that matters, not the discussing. You make your contribution to the overall musical idea by the way you carry out your part of it. That is why a really good orchestral musician is always thinking about the music, even the most familiar, and trying to improve his bit of it.

One big advantage of working in an orchestra is that your colleagues are on the whole an interesting bunch.

Musicians, like other artists, tend to have a special feeling for the unknown, the mystical, that I find is lacking in a lot of other people. This crazy slant on life seems to make them attractive. Moreover, when an orchestra is on tour there is always spare time, on buses and trains and hanging around in airports, to get to know them, something which is difficult at home base, each player taking off after work to his separate family in his separate suburb.

I say 'his', but I mean 'hers' as well. I always feel happy when there are women in an orchestra. Even just from the visual point of view, they afford relief to the serried ranks of men in their corny clothes. But I also think they give a tone of civilization which doesn't exist too much in men-only orchestras. The men-only orchestra has a sort of public bar atmosphere about it sometimes. Having women around may not remove it from the pub altogether, but at least it lifts things to saloon bar level. For these and better reasons, I think it a pity that some orchestras refuse to employ women. Not only are they good at their jobs (they have to be in our male dominated world, in which the women who succeed are extra good), but they also score, in my view, in being more conscientious and in having a wonderful quality of fantasy.

Perhaps I traduce my own sex unjustly, but such has been my experience, more particularly with students. When I was in Berlin, my male students tended to put camaraderie before practice. Turning up for a lesson they would say, 'I haven't practised this week, Jimmy. Let's go have a beer.' For a start, I didn't want a beer in the middle of the day, and secondly, if I did want one, it wouldn't be with one of my students. The women always came prepared. They were hysterical about it, but they were prepared. That was gratifying to a teacher, but beyond that I came to think that the feminine got more out of the music than did aggressive machismo masculinity. Maybe the truth of the matter is that women just drink less.

In the life of a musician there is no such thing as a Sunday. We must work, that is play, when the rest of the world is on holiday. So face the fact that as an orchestral musician your weekends will likely come mid-week when the children are at school.

The shape of your week might be something like this: rehearsal Sunday morning, concert Sunday night; a couple of recording sessions Monday; rehearsal and a concert on Tuesday; Wednesday and Thursday possibly free time unless there is a concert out of town, involving travel and a seating rehearsal; Friday perhaps another recording; Saturday you join a few others to organize a chamber music programme for the radio. I don't claim this is a typical week, because the typical orchestral week does not exist. But, rearrange the components how you like, the week tends to be crowded.

The victim of such a schedule is personal practice, more especially for those who have to fit a family life into the spaces between engagements. Daily practice remains necessary, however, for musicianship of quality. Beyond improving technique and knowing the notes, practice is about getting into the spirit of the pieces you are to play, so that at the concert the message is really put across. Practice therefore has to be done, in whatever spare half hours here and there can be contrived. In some people's view I tend to be a trifle manic about practice. They are welcome to their opinion, but I don't share it. To me, two to three hours a day are a sensible rule of life. In my orchestral days, I used to cancel some of the subsidiary engagements like recordings because I wanted to practise this or that.

Of course it is not possible for everyone to turn money down in this lighthearted fashion. In Britain orchestras are paid for what they do, piece work as it were, so that there is an inducement for players to take all the work on offer. In America I believe they are paid an annual salary, agreed before the first note of the first overture has struck. Similarly the Berlin Philharmonic pays a monthly salary which does not alter whether the musicians do ten days' work or twenty. But the Berlin Philharmonic lives on a different planet from the piece workers of Britain. It has more public money a year than all five London orchestras put together. So it can hire the most expensive musicians and get down to the pursuit of excellence in peace, quiet and security.

The difference extends to working conditions. Take travel. For local tours the Berlin Philharmonic has its own train, in which the cossetted players are forbidden to travel more than a limited number of hours a day, after which the whole train is cleaned overnight, inside and out. Meanwhile the more cumbersome instruments are taken by road with loaders to embark and disembark them. Even flutes have travelling arrangements made for them, a box with compartments tailored for the instruments of the woodwind department. At the other extreme is the under-privileged regional orchestra which never gets out of a bus except to play a concert or go to bed, and which probably humps its own instruments. When the Berlin Philharmonic travels abroad, it does things no less grandly than at home. It never travels on the same day as a concert, nor yet rehearses. Some orchestras are off the plane and into the hall with scarcely time to change.

If your future lies in an orchestra, I hope it is one at the less harassed end of the business. But anyway make the most of it. There is a great deal of pleasure in orchestral playing, if you have the right attitude to it.

Tuttis and solos

These are the two aspects of orchestral music that need the most concentrated care and attention. In the case of solos (in which I include ensemble passages too), the reason is obvious, and the musician who failed to do his homework on them would be foolish indeed. But a lot of people don't bother enough about playing tutti. Orchestral study books, focusing on the hard bits of the repertoire, sometimes leave out tuttis altogether, on the grounds presumably that the flute can't be heard very well in the general uproar and therefore how it is played is not so important. In my opinion tuttis are as important as solos.

Some are extremely difficult, simply because they go so fast and there are so many notes, all of them to be played with utter clarity and precision along with everyone else in the orchestra. Any sort of horsing around with a tutti, skipping a note here and letting a couple slide through messily there, absolutely wrecks the effect. But when the whole band is spot on and roaring along at speed, it's dramatic. That is what makes an orchestra, that's what marks off the super-excellent from the passable, and that's what has an audience jumping with adrenalin.

When I first joined the London Symphony Orchestra I could not play tuttis. Previously my orchestral experience was operatic, and though I had foreseen the need to enlarge my repertoire, I had not thought the need would arrive as suddenly as it did. So I was unprepared, with the further problem of playing a different new tune every day. I was saved by the second flute, Richard Taylor, who suggested that I stick to the solos and he would do the tuttis until I got a grip of them. There you have true team spirit, a colleague who wants you to succeed and helps you to do so. I thought it was very nice of him.

Anyone hoping to be a first flute of the future should learn from this. While you are still at college, try to get into your head a complete photograph of the whole flute part of a piece, and be spared the shock on the day.

So, one hundred per cent precision is what is required in a tutti. But your individual voice does tend to get lost in the overall sound. I used to try to overcome this by getting the second or third flute to double up with me, whatever the composer had indicated, in order to make the flute's voice twice as loud.

Getting lost in the surrounding orchestral din can also be a problem with solos. It is not impossible to have a solo passage marked *pianissimo*, accompanied by thirty people on strings. No way are those thirty strings going to play more softly than your lone flute. *Pianissimo* therefore has to be interpreted elastically, and with the strings humming away down there it must be slightly louder than if they were silent. It stands to common sense.

Solos are your moments of individual glory, when you are interpreting something on your own, usually accompanied – or with a lot of other people getting in the way, depending on how you look at it. The first thing to be done is encourage the orchestra to listen to you, which is where the flexible interpretation of *pianissimo* between you and the strings comes in. But there are limits to how loud a pianissimo can be without losing its point altogether. So you have to ask your colleagues to play as softly as possible while you put the pressure up a fraction, but still giving the illusion of playing ultra-soft. As you see, team work raises its valuable head again, even in the matter of solos.

The other thing about playing solos is the scope given for the free play of fantasy. Even if the passage is no more than a bar long – even if it is a single note – it is a chance to bring something magical to the occasion. And in longer passages, you can really take off and get lost in the music. This applies with almost equal force to ensemble playing, when a couple of instruments, for instance flute and horn, are doing the same thing two octaves apart. The freedom is only marginally less than when the flute is highlighted on its own, the musical opportunities and responsibilities just as great.

The piccolo and the alto flute

A certain versatility is required of orchestral flute players. As well as their own instrument, they are expected to be able to play, as and when needed, the piccolo, the alto flute, and possibly in extreme cases the bass flute. Usually the first flute player is spared these tasks, which get pushed down the line to the second or third or to a freelance specially hired for a piece with ambitious orchestration. In a way their job is harder than the first flute's, of whom more specialized abilities are demanded. Similarly other members of the woodwind are expected to double up on other instruments, the oboe player coping when necessary with the cor anglais or the oboe d'amore, the bassoonist with the contra-bassoon.

Clearly, mastery of the piccolo and the alto flute as well as the flute itself gives a certain advantage when competing to be taken on the orchestral strength. But unless you are fortunate in your college of music, you may have to master these additional instruments yourself.

Either way there are several things you should do.

First, with both piccolo and alto flute, make sure you have a good instrument. Secondly, find ones that have similar headpieces to that of your existing flute, so that you can use the same technique on all three. Thirdly, include these instruments in daily practice. Fourthly, learn the repertoire.

It is particularly important to devote time to practising the piccolo and its repertoire, because the instrument is difficult and a lot of the stuff written for it is very fast. Moreover every note played on it is heard with deafening clarity. The ignorant think that the bigger an instrument is, the louder it sounds, whereas the truth is pretty well the opposite. At any rate, the higher an instrument's pitch, the more exposed it is. Compare violins and double basses, or for that matter babies and adults. The smaller generally make the more noise. Any blunder on the piccolo piercingly proclaims itself.

The piccolo is an octave higher than the flute, the alto flute a fourth lower, and the bass flute an octave lower. Both alto and bass are physically larger instruments, so that it is necessary to get used to a different way of holding them and to their different weights. The repertoire tends to be specialized, a collection one might say of weird bits from weird pieces, a great many of them written by experimental twentieth-century composers who like exploiting the dark-soft sounds of these varieties of flute. To have such a repertoire under your belt makes a versatile, therefore employable, musician of you.

Nineteen
Chamber Music

The more people there are doing something, the less freedom any of them has. There is nothing like being up the mountain on your own. Composers like getting crowds together, however. Every so often a Mahler among them pops up with a *Symphony of a Thousand*, or some such thing, which demands such tremendous feats of organization that rehearsal bears a strong resemblance to a military operation. On such occasions, one gladly resigns one's freedom to the dictatorial figure of the conductor.

To be fair to conductors, they are also responsible for the overall interpretation. But both of their responsibilities – to get all these people observing the same rallentando and expressing the same musical idea – come down in the end to the question of numbers. If there are enough people engaged on an activity and only a couple of rehearsals scheduled, someone has to be boss.

Team spirit

Chamber music is a more egalitarian business altogether. Even when one of the players is foremost among equals, the chances are strong that the rallentando and the musical idea have been arrived at by the meeting of minds, if not exactly by majority vote. And the fewer people involved, the more likely it is that everything has been discussed and worked out beforehand. In other words, team spirit, which is important in symphony orchestras, is utterly vital in chamber music. But, given the small number of people involved, team spirit is more easily generated and maintained. Or if it isn't, that particular group rapidly dissolves into its component parts, who go their separate ways.

Chamber music offers both opportunities and rewards, but before coming to them I would like to knock on the head a myth about it which has gained a sort of sentimental currency. The myth is that full-time musicians like to spend their leisure by summoning colleagues from distant suburbs for a private classical jam session, rather than with the wife and children or their feet up before the television and a can of beer. The truth is, this rarely happens. Musicians, like other members of the human race, have households to keep, mortgages to pay, strength to recoup on what days off they have, and practice to be remembered somewhere in the middle of all this. In the real world local amateurs get together on a Thursday night and have a hooley rather more often than their professional counterparts.

Just occasionally professionals will indulge for the fun of it, and then it's a riot. When I was in Berlin, a student brought me a really interesting piece of chamber music: Beethoven's *Eighth Symphony* – arranged, if I remember rightly, as an octet. So I got the boys round from the orchestra and we had a bash, moving on from Beethoven to actually intended chamber music by Brahms. But usually, with orchestra professionals, a performance is in mind, say for a radio programme or something of the sort.

Chamber music is an alternative way of life to big symphony orchestras. It can still be orchestral in the proper meaning of the word, as in the English Chamber Orchestra or the Orchestra of St John's, Smith Square, where a flute or two are sometimes required. On the other hand, it may involve you in organizing your own group and trying to get some form of employment by offering your services to likely customers, for example music clubs or hotels, for some special function. Sometimes cunning is needed to enable you to play the music you fancy. Suppose, for instance, you put together a programme consisting solely of French music; a wise next step might be to seek French government sponsorship. Similarly the Arts Council or the local arts centre has been known to help subsidize worthy ventures. But, while not showing patrons the door, chamber groups should aim to create their own audience, in the interests of return engagements this year, next year and the year after. It is certainly possible to make a good career out of chamber music, and an enjoyable one.

The music

There is a wealth of beautiful pieces to be played, if somewhat unevenly spread across the history of music. To go no further back in time, the baroque era provided hundreds of works from all over Europe, followed by Bach's trio sonatas, excellent music which in the hands of the right players can really come alive and give a bit of pleasure to people. First find the people, however. Bach excepted, many of these baroque composers, good as they are, seem not to have mass audience appeal.

The flute has not been so well served in chamber music by the classical and romantic composers. Mozart, for example, wrote some great pieces for wind groups in which no flute figures, although there are the four quartets and some early sonatas. In modern times there is a whole stack of things featuring the flute, notably Debussy's *Trio* for flute, viola and harp. There is no shortage of music, nor of audiences if the music is played with the right spirit.

The rewards

I have stressed the practical problems of making a living out of chamber music, and I don't take back what I said. But we must not lose sight of the fact that music is about rejoicing. Chamber music has pleasures for the player which other sorts of music don't provide.

For a start you can enjoy yourself, because usually you play with people you like. An occasional joke is in order.

I remember one which was played on me in my early youth. My teacher, John Francis, the celebrated cellist Ambrose Gauntlet and I were rehearsing a trio for two flutes and cello, and on this particular afternoon I was last to arrive. So I come steaming in on their heels, John gives the go-ahead for the start, and we take off. The noise was indescribable. I couldn't think what was happening. 'Hey', says I, 'wait a minute, I can't get it right, I must be out of tune or something.' Light dawned when I saw their grins. Before I arrived they had fixed to play half a tone up, just to disconcert me.

More to the point, chamber music stretches the mind and imagination in a particular way. You become very much aware of the individual styles of playing, you get to know intimately the problems and the possibilities of other instrumentalists. Therefore the contact, whether in a group or a chamber orchestra is high. Not only is what any individual member says more important than in the full orchestra, but also his manner of saying it is more significant.

It could be argued that the ultimate chamber group is the string quartet. What binds a quartet together almost as closely as the marriage service is the overriding need to practise. String quartets have to have a larger repertoire than almost any other set of musicians and when they are touring an area, they can't afford to repeat themselves much. The club or society which has invited them will reject an item with the argument that they played it in the next town yesterday, or in this town last year. With all these people wanting this piece, that piece, and as a change the other piece, string quartet players really have to practise hard. I remember a quartet of fellow students, with whom I was at college, who used to practise in the room opposite me day and night till they just fell asleep in their chairs.

As a result of spending their whole time practising, string quartets get good anyway, and start to think, feel and live as a unit. For flute players the standards are not so high as in the best string quartets, because no flute player spends as much time together with another three people as a first violin and his trio. But chamber music demands of us too a very developed degree of contact with the others in the group, and we too find that, in this situation, people can be got to do things of a very special nature, not possible in a full orchestral setting.

Of all the different ways of playing music, the small group has a claim to be the best. It allows the most highly concentrated communication between a small number of individuals without a word being said. When you hear a concert of great chamber music, the players are all talking to each other with their instruments, and the whole thing is just beautifully *so*.

Twenty
Playing in a Studio

And now for something completely different. If orchestral and group playing is the permanent employment side of the job, as it were, playing in studios is strictly for temps. The engagement is a one-off, the band is put together only for the occasion, it is made up largely of freelance musicians who hire out their services here and there (some of whom may, of course, be orchestral musicians exploiting their leisure hours).

Popular music

Not only does studio playing differ in the status of the musicians, however. It also demands a whole new repertoire, or rather familiarity with twentieth century musical styles – jazz, swing, rock etc. – for which there is no great call in the symphony set-up. Furthermore, in their search for special effects, studio arrangers go in for some very bizarre instrumentation. And lastly working conditions are not the same as anywhere else.

Typical studio jobs are music for feature films, television commercials, plays and serials. The work can be well paid, but, with this commercial emphasis, the music tends not to be very interesting. People who only temp in studios may come eventually to realize that life is not taking the spiritual direction required. But not many flute players do lead such a restricted professional existence. A more common experience is to be putting the backing to *Star Wars* one day and performing Cimarosa's *Concerto for Two Flutes* the next. Doing a bit of everything can be rewarding, and I don't mean just financially. The mark of success is not to be first flute in the Berlin Philharmonic Orchestra. It is to enjoy yourself, and this can be achieved shifting around from studio to concert platform to recital hall, retaining a wide horizon.

The good thing about studios is that they offer work to a lot of people, but unfortunately the average music college doesn't equip its students for this style of playing. The Eastman School of Music in Rochester, New York State, is not an average college. In contrast to the narrow view of music fostered in British colleges, the Eastman has a department for jazz which has generated not only a big band but all sorts of little groups as well. But then the origins of the Eastman School were firmly in the entertainment world. George Eastman set it up to train pianists to accompany the silent films. He built an auditorium where they could watch the film, practising the while, and then sent them out on the road. It was a typical American management package deal. When silent films gave way to talkies, the opportunities for musicians multiplied a hundredfold of course.

Failing someone to instruct you in popular styles, you become your own instructor, and I suspect that most students have the wit to take this initiative without waiting for advice from me. Once again, the first step in the self-instruction course is to listen to records to get the sound of jazz (or whatever) into your head. The next is to play. Especially with jazz, where the rules are few and can be bent, there is no substitute for jumping in at the deep end except to listen and absorb a variety of styles.

Sight-reading

One thing the studio player has to be is a fantastic sight-reader. Just because this music is so far from the standard repertoire, you can never predict what sort of a score will be thrown at you. A daily stint to improve sight-reading is therefore another necessary preparation.

On being a flute player

What sight-reading practice does is speed up the message from the page through the brain to the fingers. In a way it is a mechanical skill, not unlike touch-typing which, although less complicated, equally involves getting the message instantaneously from (a) through (b) to (c). So you choose the piece for today's sight-reading, anything will do, say a Mozart piano sonata. Then you spy out the lie of the land, checking the key and time signatures and making sure that nothing impossible is coming up. Next you promise yourself that you are going to get to the end of the sonata without stopping, and to help you keep that promise you set off at a speed you can maintain. People like sight-reading to be done without interruptions, even if it goes a little bit wrong in the middle. When you do it wrong fifteen times, they may begin to get a little agitated, but a mistake and no pauses will pass. Over time, the exercise has to be speeded up so that an unseen stretch of notes can be played at the tempo the composer intended. When you can do that, you are ready to take on studio work.

A second instrument

However, if you are going to be hired for return engagements, or at least be really successful, it is necessary to have a second instrument to offer, the clarinet perhaps or the saxophone. Once when I was in Sydney, Australia, I went to a jazz club and heard a guy play in turn saxophone, flute, bassoon and piccolo. He was a master of all. Very rarely does one hear any individual one of these instruments played as well as he played all four. But he was somewhat above average. Such versatility is luckily not usually demanded, but proficiency on at least two instruments makes for a good living in studio work. Musicians who thus double up their chances of getting employment are called 'doublers'.

212

Playing in studios

The sound in recording studios used for film and television jobs is usually terrible. The people in charge like the acoustics to be completely dead and dry, so that this sterile sound can be souped up or have echoes put into it and otherwise be messed about with in the interests of special effects. So playing in a studio can be problematic. But here too you are required to make the most beautiful sound you can. You have to deliver the goods whatever the obstacles.

A frequent obstacle is that the overall noise level drowns out your particular voice, especially if you are playing a quiet instrument like the alto flute. Some studio players carry their own amplification just to make themselves heard, and supplying such gear is becoming increasingly common. Very few straight flute players make a living in studios these days. Straight flute playing, without doubling and without electronic dressing up, has become a thing of the past in the commercial world.

You can see that studio playing is an adventurous business, with much exploring of unknown territory involved. Actually a lot of waiting around for starters' orders can be involved too. When a symphony orchestra records something from the classical repertoire, there is a certain routine smoothness about the proceedings. For a start the orchestra has practised, rehearsed and performed the music many times. Equally important, the recording engineers know the seating lay-out of the orchestra and have the microphones properly positioned beforehand. As a result no sooner is everyone in place than the red light goes on, meaning that recording is beginning straight away. On such occasions, you have to do your practice and warming up and get your lips flexible before coming. You have to be ready to go from the minute you arrive.

In contrast, the strange orchestration dreamed up for film and television scores means that nobody knows where the mikes should go. Three-quarters of an hour may pass while they are tried out here and there. This at any rate gives you time to say hello to everybody and get yourself in playing trim.

Recording techniques are always changing, however, and it may be that, in studio work, you contribute your piece to the whole in the absence of other performers. For example, a song has perhaps been recorded, with backing, and when the tape is heard, somebody suggests a few bars of the flute in this or that passage would make all the difference. So a flute player is called in and with the tape playing does his eight or twelve bars.

I know something about these techniques, having made a record with Cleo Laine in this manner. It was my first experience of advanced recording, and I found it very interesting. The recording consisted of twenty-four channels, any one or all of which could be removed from the final master version. Some of these channels were reserved for Cleo Laine, some for me, some for other purposes. On this particular record, Cleo recorded her voice plus a bass and a click-track giving the rhythm, and on a different day entirely I went to the studio and did my bit alongside the already existing tape. If I remember rightly, I had four of the twenty-four channels, four possibilities of which the best was chosen, the others removed from the master.

Further away from a string quartet communing with itself in performance it would be hard to get. But for entertainment music, the technique works splendidly well. I enjoyed every minute of it.

Twenty-one
Soloists

Playing first flute in an orchestra is like eating cake, compared to being a soloist standing in front of the orchestra and playing a concerto. Anybody who wants to be a soloist should really think first about what sort of life they are planning to lumber themselves with.

Let's get the bad news out of the way first. Being a soloist means: being separated from your family ten months of the year; being always on the road; getting up in the wee small hours to catch a plane to some little place to amuse the population; failing to get to the little place because someone is on strike; waiting in snowed up airports in winter; putting up with hotels which can't press your suit or serve a decent breakfast; finding your health declining under these various assaults and having to do something about it. And so on and so forth. Little things in themselves, most of them, but they add up to making life just one big drag.

The truth behind the glamour is that only very very rarely do you actually get to a concert in the right state of mind. An experience of my own will make the point.

One evening I was engaged to play both the Mozart flute concertos in St Patrick's Cathedral in Dublin, and phoned for a taxi to take my wife and me there in good and tranquil time. We were standing outside the house, waiting for the taxi and admiring Dublin Bay, when I suddenly realized how late it was. To hitch a lift seemed the only option. The first driver who stopped could only take us half way into town. En route he demonstrated his new cassette recorder, all bongos and what-not, just the thing to put me in the right frame of mind for Mozart. When he threw us out, another kind fellow took us a bit further along the road, to the station, where stood a whole pile of taxis without a driver in sight. They were all in the pub. At this point I took drastic action. I walked into the middle of the road, stood in front of the first car that came along, obliged it to stop, and hijacked it to the Cathedral. As I came in, I heard the last chord of the *Siegfried Idyll*, after which it was my turn to play. I was literally straight off the street and on to the platform. Afterwards people came up and demonstrated the usual misapprehensions: 'How great to be able to get so wrapped up in a Mozart concerto!' Little did they know that all the way through the Mozart concerto I was thinking of the nastiest way, involving the maximum amount of pain and agony, of dismembering taxi drivers who fail to turn up on time.

Fortunately one gets used to things going wrong. One learns to live with it. But it is nice when, on occasion, everything operates like clockwork.

There are two very important factors to be taken into account by people considering a soloist's career. Assuming you are musically qualified for the role, you still won't gain success as a soloist unless you have, first, a special sort of contact with an audience, and, second, a good manager. Few have the first and even fewer the second. How to set about acquiring contact with audiences, I don't know. I suspect it is inborn, an aspect of personality. But if you find a good manager, what you should do is become business partners with him. The relationship should be equal, not one in which the soloist tells the manager what booking he wants, or, conversely, the manager dictates to the soloist the bookings he must take on board. The business in which both are engaged concerns bringing music to the people. To do that, you have to get a record contract organized, television appearances, and the whole publicity machine working, as well as concert tours. If you have a manager who is prepared to take all these steps, then you are half way there.

Nerves

This still leaves you in charge of the other half of the partnership, of course. It should keep you occupied. Apart from the irritations listed above, an unavoidable part of a travelling player's life, the pressures of a full engagement book can be very high. In these circumstances, sometimes you really can't do your best, some technical demands just cannot be met. The result is worry, and worry further aggravates the pressure and the problems. How should a soloist cope with nerves? The short answer is, learn not to care.

I know something about this subject, having been through the usual tribulations. When I was a boy, I didn't know about nerves, so I just went on and played regardless. Then two things happened. I began to grow up, and people started to tell me not to be nervous. Around the age of thirteen or fourteen nerves started to interfere with performance, until I took measures. You don't get nervous, I decided, if you know what you are doing, so I just stepped up the practice on things soon to be performed. Knowing that I knew the notes one hundred percent restored my calm. In orchestral playing things were a little different. I used to get nervous in the orchestra because my life depended on so many other people, but my own failings didn't disturb me overmuch. As a soloist, however, living under pressure and sometimes not matching up to my own standards, I had to work out some other way to cope. These days, if there is a tricky passage coming up which I know I can't totally guarantee, I am philosophical about it. If it goes right, okay; if it doesn't, too bad. Either way, I don't let it ruin the rest of the concert. Some poor souls would be tormented all through the performance, waiting for this bit to go wrong. Which is a sure-fire way of distracting one's attention and wasting one's emotion, not to mention ensuring that it probably *does* go wrong this time.

To recap: there are things which you are dead sure

about, so there's no need to worry; there are other things which you are not sure about, but there's no point in worrying, since you can't do anything about them. Panic is therefore an idle indulgence. Just turn up to a few concerts less than totally prepared, and you soon get used to not panicking.

But the injunction to practise long, hard and often will be observed by the wise. Apart from actually getting the music into a performable state and inspiring self-confidence, constant and lengthy practice serves a soloist in another way. It gives him the stamina to play one piece after another, each demanding concentration, for the extent of a programme. There is not much sitting around and listening to the other fellow for a soloist.

Soloist and orchestra

In general soloists divide their time between recitals with piano accompaniment and concerts with orchestra. The small repertoire for unaccompanied flute can't be relied on to carry a player through many engagements, so a very necessary part of being a soloist is the ability to get on with other people. I mean this in the specific technical sense of knowing what accompanists, orchestras and conductors can and cannot do, and fitting in with them accordingly.

During my time in orchestras the most ridiculous feats, in following and so forth, were on occasion asked of the orchestra and conductor. Such demands would be made by the sort of soloist who has spent his life to date practising in an empty room, and suddenly, as a result of some competition or another, finds himself on the platform playing a concerto with a symphony orchestra. He just doesn't know where anything's at. Therefore I think that anyone who is going to be a soloist should acquire a bit of communal background beforehand. Ideally he should have, early on, plenty of experience of both chamber and orchestral music. The problems of flute playing are quite different from those of other woodwinds, strings, brasses, and so on. But, as I have said before, successful perform-ance depends on an understanding of each other's problems and the accommodations made in consequence. The best way to get intimately acquainted with the problems of other instrumentalists is to play chamber music with them and simply by listening discover what their instruments can do. If you have already made this discovery, you are well prepared for orchestral playing, and experience here teaches the further lessons of what a conductor can do for a soloist, what a soloist can ask of an orchestra, what can be achieved in rehearsal.

What can be achieved in rehearsal is sometimes not all that much. Sometimes you are lucky if you get a rehearsal the day before, and even luckier if the same people as were at the rehearsal turn up for the concert. But, failing money enough to hire your own band and keep them at it, you must put up with the inadequate rehearsals, as currently organized. One thing rehearsals do reveal is what quality of conductor you are playing with.

There are certain conductors who take pains to know the piece in prospect, and there are others who just conduct as they go along. Which type you are teamed up with soon becomes clear, and if it proves to be the second type, not as well acquainted with the score as he might be, rehearsal gives you a chance to put across what you want to do, and arrange some sort of liaison between him, the orchestra and yourself.

As I have already said, the fewer people you make music with, the freer you are. Playing solo flute music, you can say exactly what you mean. Playing with conductor and orchestra returns you to a relative straitjacket, and if you play with the freedom dictated by your fancy you are never going to get to the finishing line. All the time a little metronome must be ticking over in your head. In the worst circumstances, there will be an orchestra of seventy people who don't know the piece, all following a conductor who has his nose in the score and hasn't yet grasped the difference between *meno mosso*, *più mosso*, or any ordinary old *mosso*. I am sorry to harp on the failings of conductors. I have known plenty of good ones. But I've also encountered the sort who can't distinguish between 120 and 124 or 128. You ask them to put it just a tiny bit faster, and they go so quick that you can't play the notes.

Personally, I often don't look at the conductor when I am playing a concerto, which doesn't mean I am trying to ignore his existence. The truth is, there is more difference than might be supposed between following the beat and actually playing in time. I have met conductors in my day who were very fierce about their beat being followed absolutely, but what was less clear was whereabouts in their gestures the beat actually was. One interpretation might have it at the top of the swing, another at the bottom. Seeing may not always be understanding, but one thing you cannot make a mistake with is your ear. Whatever the baton does, you can hear the beat, tap your foot to it, safely shut your eyes if you want.

As soloist, you are slightly more equal than the conductor when it comes to deciding the interpretation of the concerto. He is in charge of the orchestral forces but the star billing is yours. In these circumstances, it is a sad fact that composers sometimes supply so much backing for us that the flute can scarcely be heard. Klemperer used to have four flutes play Bach's *B minor Suite* in unison – and that was before he was deaf. Another trick for rescuing important phrases from the general orchestral racket is to put them up an octave. But the rule for ordinary occasions is just to remember that there is a limit to how soft you can play as a soloist. As with solo passages played by the first flute, you have to take over, be prominent, stand out from the crowd – in the interests of the music, of course, not the ego-trip which is no less unattractive in soloists than among colleagues in an orchestra.

Soloist and accompanist

A soloist's relationship with his accompanist is a good deal less hazardous and complicated, but since a lot depends upon it, it is worth knowing what sort of person you should look for. You could be embarrassed for choice, as the French say more or less, because there seem to be more piano players in the world than any other form of human life (unless maybe flute players are catching up). In the ordinary way, your first accompanists are teachers, then you move on to friends, fellow students, and so on, so that by the time you are seeking a professional you should have a wide and varied experience of accompanists and be able to tell the good from the not so good.

The not so good depend on sight-reading ability, or if they have practised their own chords a few times, they sight-read the flute part as they go along. The really good accompanist naturally plays the piano very well, but not only that. He listens, studies the flute part, knows the difficult bits, is prepared to rehearse long enough to check out all these things and put them right, and is generally a model of patience, flexibility and sympathy. Just such a model is my friend and accompanist Phillip Moll.

In this relationship the soloist too has responsibilities. Most music for this sort of situation is not for soloist and accompanist, but for two instruments in communication with each other, communication which may be passionate, witty, soulful, light-hearted, but whatever else it is, it is shared. The two of you have to be together, one intelligence, united souls incorporated. The flute has to become the third line of the piano. And this takes effort, musicianship, and hours and hours of work to bring off. So another thing to make sure of is that the accompanist is going to stay around that long.

Soloist and audience

There is one further human factor which a soloist has to take into account: the audience. Unlike pianists, whose furniture gets between them and the listeners, a flute player engages the audience directly. It can be very interesting to

221

watch an audience while one plays, so it is a good first idea to play *to* the people, rather than to the light fixtures or the fly on the wall. There is a story about a violinist facing his first concerto and nervous about it, who was advised to shut his eyes, imagine himself back home, and just play. Unfortunately he was one of these overactive musicians whose bodies dance to the tune. When he opened his eyes at a suitable break in the proceedings, he found himself facing the orchestra with the audience at his back. If you want to cut the cord of communication, this is surely the way to go about it.

But a musician has to regard his audience in another way than simply looking it in the eye. The musician's chief duty is to entertain. This word has lost caste in recent years. Entertainment is considered something rather low, for the masses all the time and for the top people only in their time off. But I don't take back the word. Entertainment should not be played down. I don't deny that music can be profound, touch deepest emotions, express things beyond the power of words, but its greatest achievements are arrived at only by its power to delight. People don't quit home comforts for lectures on music, they come for the music itself, because they enjoy it, because it is entertaining.

So a soloist who plans to give the people what they want to hear is not stuck with the lowest common denominator of the easily digestible. He has all the classical pops at his disposal. That said, it has to be acknowledged that audiences vary and there is such a thing as a minority taste. At the Edinburgh Festival, for example, you can be confident of an audience of initiates, who are into the hard stuff, as it were, and will not blench if something obscure is served up to them. With more randomly collected audiences, my own plan is to move from the more demanding to the less, in the course of a concert. So in the first half of the programme there might be the Nielsen concerto or the Prokofiev Sonata, followed after the interval by something instantly accessible, such as transcriptions of Kreisler's encores. As with nursery supper, the nutritious stuff comes first, and soufflé afterwards, but both first course and second are designed to please.

In this practice, I am proud to follow the precedent set by Fritz Kreisler. He was one of the greatest violinists of this century, whose recording of the Beethoven *Violin Concerto* remains a milestone, but he never disdained his role as entertainer. After a regular sonata programme he would play delightful little tunes, many composed by himself, to send the audience home whistling.

Transcriptions

My homage to Kreisler goes beyond programme planning to playing transcriptions of the music he wrote for the violin. I am an unashamed transcriber, and have received not a little flak on that account from purists who seem to have a sort of bureaucratic approach to music and frown upon transcribing pieces written for one instrument for performance on another. The idea is that everything has its proper place and no actual performing entertainer should be allowed to upset the filing system. What these scholarly critics overlook is that transcription is an ancient custom, practised by some very respectable names. While Vivaldi was still alive, the first movement of *The Four Seasons*, written for solo violin and strings, was arranged for solo flute. Bach made many transcriptions of Vivaldi's works, Handel – as I have mentioned – transcribed anything from anywhere if it caught his fancy. Nearer our own day Rachmaninov even arranged our own *Dance of the Blessed Spirits* for the piano and what is more made a record of the transcription.

If composers of that stature can get away with it, why can't we? To my mind it is an excellent way to give music back to the people, to get them switched on to the subject and extend their knowledge of it. I think young people in school should play the music they actually enjoy, instead of the possibly boring pieces thrown at them in college syllabuses, and if that means transcribing, well, hooray for them. Another thing I am accused of, quite rightly, is transcribing modern popular music, songs by John Denver for example, and putting this type of music into programmes along with the all-time respected greats. I make no apology. But I do refuse to have pigeon-holes for filing music in.

Transcription not only gets the music to the people, it also enlarges the repertoire of the flute, which is an important consideration for a soloist. People have made the grade without playing transcriptions, but by opting to stick to the old respected classics they have not brought as much good music to as wide an audience as they might otherwise have done. Much flute music frankly belongs in a museum, more notable for its antiquity than its quality, possibly rather academically boring and completely uninspired. I think one is better advised to leave the museum pieces to the historian and transcribe something which has some musical inspiration.

Fortunately for soloists and audiences, a lot of music has already been transcribed for the flute by musicians who shared my enthusiasm for the operation. But a lot has to be done by oneself. In this case, you start by basing your effort upon what others have done, learning from their example and getting better as you go along. Personally I make myself responsible for the flute part and generally get help with the orchestration, because actually writing the whole thing out is a painful process. But I give myself the privilege of making suggestions, for example, not to have the first violins doubling with the flute in a certain passage, or to have the strings do a few bars pizzicato, or to put the bassoon in here or there. For beginners the violin repertoire is a good place to look for transcribable material, given the similar range of the instruments. True, the violin goes higher and lower, but one can always transpose up or down an octave. Moreover composers have given the violin good tunes.

One piece which I am popularly supposed to have

'stolen' is the Mozart *Clarinet Concerto*. In fact I only arranged a few bits in it that I thought could bear improvement. The main transcription was actually done in Mozart's time, by Mr Müller, the man who prepared Mozart's compositions for publication, and his reason was a good commercial one. Mozart wrote the concerto for a 'basset-clarinet', on which an acquaintance of his happened to perform outstandingly well – an instrument not much played then or since. So Mr Müller, intending to sell what he published, arranged the piece for the clarinet and for the flute besides, and his manuscript is in the East Berlin library to this day.

Commissioning music

A hazard of a successful soloist's life is the unsolicited manuscript, hopefully posted off to him by aspiring composers who want to climb on board the bandwagon. In my own experience nothing which posterity can't afford to miss has so far reached me by this channel. But involvement in new music offers genuine pleasures, one of them being the creative company of composers. It is rewarding to work with composers of different lands and to find out what they are up to in the cause of the advancement of music. One method of accomplishing this is to commission work.

My first commission had encouraging results. I asked Edwin Roxburgh to compose some cadenzas for a Mozart flute concerto, and won a competition with the piece. Later I discovered the drawbacks to commissioning. For a start, composers of serious music are on the whole extremely expensive. The time has gone when a composer would sit down and write something for nothing. In Haydn's day, things were different, but Haydn was one of the pop stars of his time, and he could be confident that what he wrote would have the cash registers tinkling. Today serious composers don't generally write music of wide appeal, so they write in response to a commission more often than not, in the interests of paying the rent. As a result they cost a lot, and anyone planning a commission has first to get financial backing from somewhere.

Sometimes organizations will invite an artist to participate in a joint operation, which takes care of the finance. For example the BBC asked Thea Musgrave to write a piece, and me to play it. Our collaboration in the BBC's experimental studios brought *Orfeo 1*, for flute and quadrophonic tape, into existence. Later a ballet was choreographed to the music. Another possibility ensuring that the composer gets paid out of someone else's pocket is the commission for an event. I was to have participated in such a performance at the Hollywood Bowl on American Independence Day, 1980. The composer was John Corigliano, who was commissioned to write a flute concerto and came up with the idea of basing it on Robert Browning's poem, *The Pied Piper*.

As may be imagined, this concerto gives the flute a chance to shine, and a nice theatrical touch was added to its charms when, towards the end of the piece, prearranged children in the audience began to leave their seats, drawn by the piper's melody on to the platform and off-stage in his wake. In the event John was seriously ill; the work was postponed and was premiered in Los Angeles eighteen months later.

But another problem about commissioning is that you never know what a composer is going to turn up with. It could be simple to play, or fiendishly difficult. It might be a real contribution to music or something you could as easily leave as take. One time in Paris Rubinstein was looking after Stravinsky, who was on his uppers, and thought he might get the piano concerto of the century as a goodbye present. He did receive a new work but was disappointed when he opened the package and discovered Stravinsky's newly composed Piano Rags. Then again, you never know what sort of appeal a commissioned work is going to have for the public. Of course you take precautions. You do a reconnaissance first of likely composers, and make your application to the one whose work you like. This is what I did before commissioning the *Concierto Pastoral* from Joaquín Rodrigo. He produced a really fine work, but I have to warn you that there just isn't another piece that hard.

One last word on the soloist's place in the general scheme of things: that word is competition. You may be wondering just what sort of a cut-throat rat-race all we flute soloists exist in. In my experience competition doesn't arise. For orchestral jobs, yes; for soloists, no. The soloist creates his own audience, his own market, so success or failure depends on his ability to do this, not on competing with somebody else for bookings. He doesn't take work away from other musicians, but rather creates new job opportunities for orchestras and for colleagues by inviting them to appear with him on television shows and so forth. For everybody who makes the grade, there is work enough.

Twenty-two

The Flute Today and Tomorrow

The flute player of today and tomorrow is fortunate. With the business expanding in so many directions, there is a place for many different sorts of playing, one or several of which may carry him to fame, happiness and moderate prosperity.

Contemporary music

But the flute player of today and tomorrow is not, in my view, as fortunate as all that. Many modern composers, not content with the charm of a well played flute, insist on putting players through a whole range of experimental hoops. We must be careful of course about condemning *avant-garde* composers – after all, Weber once said that Beethoven was 'ripe for the madhouse' – but there is no denying that a good deal of contemporary music is nearly as hard to listen to as it is to play, and that's very hard indeed. There is a minority audience for it, but with the demand so small I don't feel obliged to go in for it. That doesn't mean that I don't play any contemporary music. I do, I even commission it, but I don't play any music that I don't believe in.

However, I have good news for you and the rest of the Western world. I think that, even among progressive composers, tunes may be coming back in. Certainly the contemporary music I admire and want to play reflects the past in some way (not many people have a past in bubble-and-squeak). The novelty of all those wild experiments of the 1970s has worn off, and composers seem now to realize that the market does not favour the ultra-subjective and idiosyncratic, that human beings actually prefer the *Pastoral Symphony* or *Eine Kleine Nachtmusik* – which are full of good tunes. For example John Mayer's flute concerto, *Mandala Ki Raga Sangeet* (a circle of raga music), is thoroughly of the twentieth century, not a pastiche of the past, but it is tuneful. John Mayer is an Indian, and once when he was in Calcutta he heard a beggar singing a traditional begging song. Immediately he wrote down the tune and incorporated it, in the form of variations on a theme, into the concerto. I like music to be connected to the past in this sort of way: a new creation, but not a rootless one.

So I pin some of my hopes for the future on the rediscovery by composers that the flute is an instrument of great expressiveness and beauty which can still attract and move large numbers of people.

Recording

This said, the electronic revolution is not going to go away, and nor are all the new things to do on a flute which electronics have made possible. I shall get round to the fancy work in a moment or two. Meanwhile let's start with the most established of electrical devices, straightforward recording.

A record is a very extraordinary thing when you come to think of it. On the whole records have become such a normal part of life that we never *do* think about how extraordinary they are. I invite you to contemplate the marvel for a minute. It seems that the feeling of a person's soul can be recorded. For example, my heroine Maria Callas is dead, but her voice on a gramophone record still has the power to move a listener to tears. What is it that gets recorded, her voice, or something more?

Whatever it is, it survives studio conditions. Perhaps nothing can equal the excitement of the live concert, but a recording is very far from a dead occasion. Playing for an audience is an event, playing for records is the event encapsulated for the great buying public and posterity. That is how I like to organize things, anyway, and I have had my share of experience in the matter: the Berlin Philharmonic was a sort of recording assembly line, never off the job. Nowadays I try to arrange for a recording to be made of music prepared for, say, a tour, so that I have ten performances maybe, not to mention practice and rehearsals, under my belt before entering the studio. Such a degree of preparation makes for quick despatch on the day.

Personally I don't check all the takes myself. I know when things have gone right or wrong, without waiting to hear the takes played back. But the chance of having two or more shots at a piece is definitely an advantage of recorded music, the more so as the good bits from one tape can be married with the good bits from another to make a satisfactory performance which never in fact existed. There's a sobering thought. Sometimes when I do a take, I think to myself, oh ho! a wrong note there! but may still prefer to commit this version to the disc because it has some other quality, some sparkle or *joie de vivre*, that seems to me more important than clinical perfection. There are musicians who, in the pursuit of perfection, do more takes than you would believe. I think two takes of anything are generally enough. Once the records are safely in the can, I never listen to them.

Playing with recorded tapes

Recording has moved on from being simply a way of serving up music in multiple copies to being a musical technique in its own right. It replaces the chamber orchestra or piano, for example, as accompaniment to a solo instrument. What attracts composers is the godlike power to invent all sorts of space-age sounds which taped music and synthesizers have made available to them. Instead of being restricted to flutes and violins, they record flutes and violins and treat them electronically, quite often turning them into something totally unrecognizable. I have mentioned the piece which the BBC commissioned Thea Musgrave to compose and me to play on this principle. Another time when I played a piece for flute and tape recorder the outcome was not so happy.

The problem was that this was a live concert, with no chance of double takes of any variety. The piece in question was *Cadence V* by Lazarof. The scene was Berlin. Before the concert I practised thoroughly with my neighbour upstairs, a very nice fellow who couldn't read music but was well able to turn on a tape recorder and from our session together knew just when to do it. Came the show. I squeaked out a few notes, the signal for him to do his stuff, and nothing happened. I kept going and nothing continued to happen. Still busily playing away, I looked round and out of the corner of my eye saw my friend making SOS gestures from the wings. I stopped then and said, 'Ladies and gentlemen, until we get our act together behind here, I'm afraid I shall have to play something more old-fashioned.'

The technical hitch on this occasion was the cleaning lady's little boy. The tape recorder had been left in concert readiness in the afternoon, when in came the lady and the lad who switched one switch, the one operating the capstan. My friend in the wings there was turning the on-off button frantically, he could hear the engine was running, but the capstan and therefore the tape just failed to go round.

This experience rather sunk electronic music in my regard. Even when it is appealing or interesting, and some of it is, there are just too many things to go wrong. Also there is the question of expense. Not so much the vast sums demanded for me and my tape recorder, but the truly colossal expense involved in setting up the sort of amplified sound environment used in popular music these days. I once met a folk singer whose act consisted of herself plus guitar. As troubadours went, she must travel light, I observed. Don't you believe it, she replied: the assembling and disassembling of the stage, the lighting and amplification, and the transporting of all this gear came to thousands of pounds a night! You have to make a fair profit to absorb costs like that.

The ultimate in electronic treatment of sound is probably to be found in the Beaubourg Centre in Paris, at the Institut de Recherche et Coordination Acoustique/ Musique, known for short by the inelegant acronym IRCAM. Here composers work, alongside performers and technicians, in a welter of computer terminals, digital recording facilities, and complicated devices for generating and changing sound. The laboratory has replaced the music room. IRCAM was launched in the early 1970s on a wave of grandiose claims, adding up in brief to the promise that music would never be the same again. So far the promise remains unfulfilled, perhaps because so few musicians know how to use computers, and IRCAM has become just another electronic music studio although an immensely sophisticated one. It is too soon to write it off as uncreative, but it will be interesting to see whether my prophecy that tunes are coming back wins out, or whether the high jinks at the Beaubourg Centre have much of a future. I know what I think.

Modern gadgets

Electronics have made it possible to use the flute in ways never dreamed of by our forebears. Essentially the gadgets are the electronic microphone, amplification equipment, and tapes which can be treated as described above. The appeal of the techniques which these gadgets allow is mainly felt by experimental musicians, of either the advanced jazz or the advanced serious variety. You are pretty sure to encounter music of these styles, later if not sooner.

One of the effects produced electronically is playback.

By means of a reverberation device in the amplification equipment, whatever you play is played back one second or a micro-second later, thus putting an echo into the sound and giving it an extra dimension.

But microphones remain a problem. This does not apply to straightforward recordings of the flute's standard repertory, for on those occasions it is the sound in the studio or concert hall that is being recorded. But for the purposes of experimental music, the flute plays directly into the microphone. Experience of this teaches one just how difficult it is to mike a flute. The reason lies in the way the instrument is played. Unlike an oboe or clarinet player, we don't blow all the air into the instrument, some of it escapes round the edges, and a certain amount of this extraneous noise, not heard in ordinary performance, is picked up by the electronic microphone. Moreover, low notes emerge from a different part of the flute from high ones, so in this cheek-by-jowl-by-microphone intimacy, there is no perfect place for the mike. And that is if you stand still. If you shift around six inches or so, the microphone pick-up changes completely. The celebrated American jazz flute player, Hubert Laws, goes in for modern gadgetry. When last seen, he was experimenting with a miniature electronic mike clipped on to the head joint, so that it was projecting just above his mouth and moved around with him.

Perhaps digital recording will take care of the extraneous noise problem. Digital recording processes sound into figures, and any unwanted figures representing bumps, scratches, coughs, oaths, and presumably extraneous hiss can simply be subtracted from the total on the master version. Old records put through the digital recording treatment come out as good as new.

Some players make a virtue of necessity, however, and actually use the faint hiss of the escaping air as a component of the performance. To play with the extraneous noise, along with the true tone of the flute, is their chosen technique.

On being a flute player

There is a whole range of cute tricks to be brought off with electronic help. Some players sing while they blow. Some whistle. To get a whistle tone, you put a piece of Scotch tape over the sides of the embouchure and without actually blowing the flute, you can make a very loud whistling noise into a microphone. Others again, or it might be the same pioneer on another occasion, click the keys. In this technique the amplified sound of the impact is the note: the flute as percussion instrument. Or the headpiece can be taken off and the player blow, hum, sing or whistle through the open end. Or simply move his finger in and out of the headpiece, with results that fail to rock the world in my opinion. It seems that practically anything can be done with a flute nowadays, other than work on it for a nice tone.

For all these experiments, amplification is needed. Amplification boils down basically to how much money you want to spend. Buy a cheap amp, and your flute will just sound loud. Buy a really expensive amplifier, and you can get it to sound beautiful as well. If you can't afford the best, it remains a bad idea to invest in the worst. I think three quarters of the reason why the average parent dislikes popular music is that the general run of amplification is so bad.

Circular breathing

Classical music makes allowance for the respiratory system of flute players, if not always allowance enough. There are usually natural spaces for breathing, and with practice one learns not to sound like a vacuum cleaner at the last gasp. But other sorts of music, ancient and modern, make no allowance whatever. The technique adopted here is what is called 'circular' or 'continuous' breathing.

Glassblowers use this method of breathing, so do Australian Aborigines for playing the didgeridoo, and so do Indian flute players. The drones in an Indian band have to keep up one note for three hours maybe, accompanying variegated other flutes, and all without pause to take a lungful. Jazz players have brought the technique back into fashion in the West. Hubert Laws, for example, can keep up *Amazing Grace* for five minutes without taking a breath. How is it done?

Not easily, is the true reply. Circular breathing requires one to breathe out and in at the same time, a feat which the human breathing equipment was not designed to achieve and which therefore demands ingenuity and practice to bring off. The idea is that you breathe in through the nose while breathing out through the mouth. Try it for complexity, and you will gain a whole new admiration for glassblowers, didgeridoo players and the like. The common way to train yourself to work against nature is to get a tumbler of water and a straw, and strive to blow bubbles through the straw while the nose breathes in.

Failing this real, genuine method of circular breathing, there is another technique. A quantity of breath is conserved in the cheeks, and this reserve supply is used to blow, while a quick breath is seized through the nose; whereupon the reserve supply is topped up again, and so ad infinitum, if that is what is scheduled. But this technique isn't easy, either. With lesser practitioners of either method, some squeak or gurgle can generally be heard between the simultaneous ins and outs.

Circular breathing sounds funny when used for music not intended for it, and it makes audiences uncomfortable. They keep waiting for the trick to collapse. This sort of tension occasionally has its uses, however. There is a recording of a live concert in which Hubert Laws not only gives a fantastic display of circular breathing, but also bends the note up very slowly, sliding up towards the semitones. It is so clever and so tense and goes on so long that finally a member of the audience can't take any more and yells 'Help!' or 'Wow!' or some other appreciative comment.

On being a flute player

Improved flutes

We should end, I think, where we began, with the instrument itself.

There is no question that the standard of flutes has improved enormously in recent years, nor that much of the credit for the improvement belongs to Albert Cooper of Britain, who has had a chapter to himself. In the 1960s a few players, such as William Bennett and myself, actually played Mr Cooper's instruments, took them round, demonstrated that they were in fact better than anything else available, and generally spread the gospel. Other instrument makers caught on, notably the Japanese, who like to succeed in business.

By Mr Cooper and his disciples the flute has been improved virtually to the limit. For the job it is required to do by the existing repertoire, it is really the optimum instrument. But, as we have seen, the job description is always expanding, and for new demands, a new flute or flutes will have to be designed.

One current attempt to build a flute to new job specifications is being made by Robert Dick. He is developing an instrument to enable him to play multiphonics or double-stopping, which the existing flute is frankly not very good at. Robert Dick's specially built flute will make double-stopping easier and more in tune.

There is one technical improvement to the standard flute which I would like to see made. That is, better pads to the keys. As some of you may have noticed, the traditional pad, made of felt and skin, is susceptible to atmospheric change, and according to the dampness or dryness of the air will swell or shrink, moving around a little bit and sometimes failing to seal the hole perfectly. So now is the time for some genius to come up with a good artificial plastic pad that really works. Get to it, inventors.

With or without better pads, the flute has a future which promises to be as lively, varied and interesting as its past.

Ours has always been a popular instrument, more

popular than the general public has perhaps always noticed. There have always been kids learning the flute, an army of them, until they get diverted into other paths. The flute is attractive not least because a technique can be worked up on it more easily than on some instruments, but also because few instruments are so flexible and diverse.

Maybe in the past it did not have as much public exposure as it has today. It so happened that the taste of people who ran radio stations tended to favour piano and violin players above other instrumentalists, the result being a glut of violins and pianos on classical music programmes. But what the classical fellows downgraded, the subversive world of jazz began to supply from around the 1950s. Next the mystical side of the flute, with its connections to Hindu and Buddhist philosophy, began latterly to draw the crowds. Simultaneously, early instruments such as the one-keyed flute and the baroque flute were resurrected from the museums to play the music written for them. Some performances on these early flutes are really impressive nowadays.

So the flute has taken off in half a dozen directions. No matter which you follow there is music and, very likely, an audience at the end of it. But the important thing, whether you play classical or jazz, romantic or experimental, baroque or Indian, is that you get a kick out of it. And that goes even if you don't play so well as yet. Have fun with the flute.

Discography and Repertoire

A number of books in this series have concluded with both repertoire lists and discographies. It seems to me that a library is the best place to discover flute music and for a fairly definitive list you should consult Frans Vester's catalogue, which is both comprehensive and excellent.

Either the current *Gramophone* or *Schwann* Catalogues will tell you which flute records are available so that I do not need to list them here. Many excellent and interesting flute records have been made and I leave you to listen to them and make up your own mind as to their musical value. I would, however, urge you to acquire the complete boxed set of recordings by the great Marcel Moyse which was compiled by the Muramatsu Flute Company.

Most important, I believe, is to listen to any and every recording of Maria Callas, Jascha Heifetz, Vladimir Horowitz and Artur Rubinstein. These are four of the great musicians of all time and I personally have gained an incalculable amount of musical insight from listening to their records – to say nothing of the pure joy of the experience.

Index

Index

Index

Index